# Cambridge Elements ≡

Elements in Criminology
edited by
David Weisburd
*George Mason University, Virginia*
*Hebrew University of Jerusalem*

# CRIME DYNAMICS

## *Why Crime Rates Change Over Time*

Richard Rosenfeld
*University of Missouri – St. Louis*

**CAMBRIDGE**
UNIVERSITY PRESS

Shaftesbury Road, Cambridge CB2 8EA, United Kingdom

One Liberty Plaza, 20th Floor, New York, NY 10006, USA

477 Williamstown Road, Port Melbourne, VIC 3207, Australia

314–321, 3rd Floor, Plot 3, Splendor Forum, Jasola District Centre, New Delhi – 110025, India

103 Penang Road, #05–06/07, Visioncrest Commercial, Singapore 238467

Cambridge University Press is part of Cambridge University Press & Assessment, a department of the University of Cambridge.

We share the University's mission to contribute to society through the pursuit of education, learning and research at the highest international levels of excellence.

www.cambridge.org
Information on this title: www.cambridge.org/9781009454049

DOI: 10.1017/9781009420365

First published 2024

*A catalogue record for this publication is available from the British Library.*

ISBN 978-1-009-45404-9 Hardback
ISBN 978-1-009-42033-4 Paperback
ISSN 2633-3341 (online)
ISSN 2633-3333 (print)

# Crime Dynamics

## Why Crime Rates Change Over Time

Elements in Criminology

DOI: 10.1017/9781009420365
First published online: May 2024

Richard Rosenfeld
*University of Missouri – St. Louis*

**Author for correspondence:** Janet L. Lauritsen, janet_lauritsen@umsl.edu

**Abstract:** This Element reviews and augments research on changes over time in US crime rates during the past several decades. Major topics include the data sources for studying crime trends; the relationship between homicide rates and rates of property crime, imprisonment, and firearm availability; trends in crime by sex, race, and age; the relationship between crime trends and economic conditions; crime trends and social institutions; abrupt changes in crime rates and exogenous shocks; forecasting crime rates; and the future of crime trends theory and research. The study of crime trends is as intellectually rewarding and practically important as any topic in criminology. But attracting scholars to this field of study of crime trends will require significant advancements in theory, methods, and policy application.

**Keywords:** crime trends, homicide trends, crime and social institutions, forecasting crime rates, crime trends and exogenous shocks

ISBNs: 9781009454049 (HB), 9781009420334 (PB), 9781009420365 (OC)
ISSNs: 2633-3341 (online), 2633-3333 (print)

# Contents

# Memoriam

## Richard Rosenfeld
(1948–2024)

Richard Rosenfeld was one of the most important and impactful criminologists of the last half century. He was recognized as a leading light of criminological theory and research by his receipt of the Sutherland Award in 2017, the most important honor for criminologists in the United States. But he was also elected as president of the American Society of Criminology in 2010, suggesting that he was not only one of America's leading criminologists, he was also respected for his leadership of criminology as a discipline. For me, Rick was simply one of the most thoughtful people I ever worked with. He was always on the cutting edge, and always asking questions that we hadn't answered yet, and in some cases had not even thought about. I served with Rick on the Crime Trends workshop he chaired of the National Academy of Sciences which is where I saw how far ahead he was of traditional criminologists in his thinking about predicting crime trends. His decision to include me on the workshop, was itself an innovation, since I had not really done much work in this area. But Rick saw the study of place at the micro geographic level as a new way of thinking that could add insight into how traditional crime trends researchers understood patterns over time. Again, Rick was on the cutting edge exploring the boundaries of what we knew and could know. This Element developed out of this life long interest of Rick's. I asked him if he would be willing to produce an Element that would summarize what we knew and suggest where we ought to be going in trying to understand crime trends. I was excited when he jumped on the idea, and told me that he had been thinking about this and wanted to go ahead with writing something. The result is this Element, which lays out a turning point in understanding crime trends, which only someone with Rick's long history of leadership in this area could have produced. Suggesting how important Rick saw the Element, he completed it shortly before his passing. We are enriched by his commitment to telling this story. "May his memory be a blessing."

# 1 Why Study Crime Trends?

We begin with a question: What is the crime rate? Not the definition of the crime rate (crimes divided by population) but the rate itself? How about the violent crime rate? The property crime rate? These are not rhetorical or trick questions; they have answers. Here they are: In 2020 the US violent crime rate was about 398 violent crimes per 100,000 population, the property crime rate was about 1,958 property crimes per 100,000, and the total crime rate was 2,356 crimes per 100,000, the sum of the violent and property crime rates.[1] I suspect most readers, even many social scientists, did not know the answers or even come close to them. Had I asked about the unemployment rate or inflation rate, however, many more readers would surely have come closer to the mark (about 3% and 6% at this writing). Why is the crime rate different?

Part of the answer is that most people think the crime rate, whatever it is, is always higher than it should be. Not so with unemployment and inflation. Labor market rigidities, stagnation, and other economic ailments brew when these conditions drop below a certain level. The US Federal Reserve and the central banks of other nations set these low points and do what they can to keep unemployment and inflation above them. We have an interest, therefore, in knowing the rates of these economic indicators so that we can tell whether they portend trouble, when they are too low as well as when they are too high. Because most people believe the crime rate can never be too low, there is no anchor point that gives it underlying value or meaning. All most of us really want to know about the crime rate is whether it is going up or down. While there are good reasons, discussed later, to worry when crime rates dip below their "normal" levels, the belief that what really matters about crime rates is how they are changing has a good deal of truth to it.

Crime is an inherently dynamic phenomenon. It moves over time and across space. We can take a snapshot of the crime rate at a single point in time and compare it with snapshots of other conditions at the same time; that is how most research on crime is done. These static pictures are not without merit, but they can be as misleading as a frozen smile in a photograph. Moving pictures provide a more complete and accurate portrayal of how crime alters and is altered by the rhythms of social life. The practitioner concerned with crime almost always turns to the question of change: What policy, strategy, or procedure can I change to reduce crime? To answer that question, the evidence-based practitioner must look to theory and research on change over time in crime rates.

---

[1] The crime rates are based on offenses known to the police and are from the FBI's Crime Data Explorer (https://crime-data-explorer.app.cloud.gov/pages/explorer/crime/crime-trend).

The study of crime rates has a venerable history in criminology. It emerged from the sociological positivism of the nineteenth century in the pioneering statistical analyses of crime and suicide rates by Quetelet, Guerry, and Durkheim. It assumes that crime is a fundamentally social phenomenon that should be investigated using the logic and statistical methods of the natural sciences. That said, Quetelet's and Guerry's research designs were predominantly cross-sectional (Donnelly 2016; Whitt and Reinking 2002). They were struck by the constancy of crime rates over time and their variability across place. By contrast, Durkheim's conception of anomic suicide linked suicide rates to the disruptive consequences of social change (Durkheim 1951[1897]). All of the early moral statisticians, however, were united in the belief that crime is a social fact, a patterned regularity of social life, and should be analyzed in relation to other social facts. Without these fundamentals, the study of crime trends would be unrecognizable.

The idea that crime is a "social fact," an attribute of a social system and not just of individuals, may strike some readers as overly abstract. But changes in crime over time have concrete consequences for both individuals and communities. The reasons seem obvious but are worth stating explicitly. The kinds of predatory crimes that are the focus of this Element constitute significant individual and social harms. They result in death, serious injury, and trauma. They deprive individuals of their liberty, property, and sense of security and safety. They cause fear. At high levels, they can destabilize entire communities. When predatory crime, especially violence, increases, politicians and pundits often use fear to win votes and promote policies, such as mass incarceration, that may do more harm than good. Crime trends have consequences, in other words, that everyone, not just criminologists, should care about.

## 1.1 Contents of the Element

*Crime Dynamics* considers many of the major theoretical and empirical contributions of the criminologists, sociologists, historians, and economists who have sought to explain the sources of change in crime rates. This study, like most crime trends research, is avowedly macroscopic in orientation. The focus is on crime trends in nations, cities, regions, and other large subnational units during the past several decades. Some potentially relevant topics, developmental and life-course research on individual change in criminal behavior, for example, are not covered comprehensively or are omitted. The Element also focuses on trends in street crime, primarily homicide, in the United States. Comparable data on trends in corporate, white-collar, and online crime do not exist, and homicide is the most serious, best measured, and most frequently studied criminal offense in the crime trends research literature. Comparable studies of crime trends in other nations are left to others.

The sections in this Element cover the major data sources in the study of crime trends; the impact on violent crime of property crime, the prevalence of firearms, and imprisonment; the demography of crime trends; the relationship between crime and the economy; crime trends and institutional change; exogenous shocks that produce large and unexpected changes in crime rates; forecasting future crime rates; and where crime trends theory and research should go from here. Section 2 describes the most widely used sources of data in the study of crime trends. Some data sources are based on offenses recorded by police departments. Others are from public health sources and surveys of crime victims. Most of the data are collected and disseminated by government agencies, but data compiled by private entities play an increasingly prominent role in recent crime trends research. Each data source has strengths and limitations, and the different sources are best viewed as complementary rather than incompatible.

Section 3 discusses three sources of change in violent crime: property crime, firearms, and imprisonment. While some prominent criminologists have argued that property crime has little or no effect on violent crime, and homicide in particular, the section subjects this contention to critical scrutiny and offers reasons why the sheer volume of property crimes should be expected to exert a sizable influence on criminal violence. There is little dispute that homicide is related to the availability of firearms. More controversial, inside and outside of criminology, is whether widespread access to firearms increases or reduces rates of homicide and other violent crimes. The relationship between crime and imprisonment trends is also controversial. Recent research suggests that increases in imprisonment probably result in decreases in crime rates, but the effects generally are small and diminish even further at high levels of imprisonment.

Section 4 examines differences in crime trends by race, ethnicity, and gender. It may come as some surprise that the crime trends among males and females and in the Black, White, and Hispanic populations are quite similar. What distinguishes these groups is their *level* of crime, not the *change* in their crime rates over time. This could mean that the common group trends are a consequence of common causes. Not all group-specific crime trends are the same, however. For example, this section presents evidence that intimate-partner homicide has declined more rapidly over time among males than females.

Section 5 considers the relationship between crime trends and changes in the age composition of the population. Street crime rates peak in the late teens and early twenties. As the adolescent and young adult segment of the population grows, as it did during the 1960s and 1970s resulting from the "baby boom" after the Second World War, crime rates turn up. As the baby boom cohorts were replaced by smaller age cohorts in the 1980s, crime rates came down. But not for long. Crime rates rose again beginning in the late 1980s, even as the size of the youthful population continued to decline. Changes in the size of this population place upward or downward pressure on crime rates, but other factors often outweigh the effect on crime trends of changes in the age composition of the population. Just as the size of age cohorts matters for crime trends, so does when the cohorts were born. Cohorts born at different times can differ in their current crime rates, quite apart from the effects of age or other current conditions. The influence on crime rates of the circumstances of birth and early development is an indispensable part of the story of why crime rates move up and down over time.

Research on the impact of economic conditions on crime rates is as old as the study of crime trends itself. Section 6 discusses the evolution of this research from early studies of the relationship between crime trends and the business cycle, to investigations of the effects of unemployment on crime rates, to recent research on how crime rates respond to changes in consumer sentiment and inflation. This is one of the most stimulating and important areas of inquiry in the study of crime trends because it bridges the theoretical interests and methodological tools of economists and criminologists, and it necessarily directs attention to policy and institutional realms well beyond the criminal justice system.

To this point, *Crime Dynamics* covers the data and much of the research on crime trends, but stops short of asking what it all means. What are the underlying structures, processes, and mechanisms that help to make sense of the disparate demographic, social, and economic influences on crime trends discussed thus far? In short, is there a *theory* of crime trends? Section 7 presents the outlines of such a theory that is rooted in what has been termed the "new institutionalism" in criminology. Social institutions are the guideposts of society. Institutional structure, regulation, and performance shape the incentives, opportunities, and constraints that result in both long- and short-run changes in crime rates over time.

Not all sources of change in crime rates are knowable in advance. On occasion crime rates change abruptly without prior warning. No one to my knowledge predicted the Covid-19 pandemic or the effects, which turned out to be quite complex, it would have on crime rates. Section 8 discusses the impact on crime rates of such "exogenous shocks" and how they elude the conventional explanatory tools of crime trends research. Exogenous shocks not only upset "normal science" studies of past crime trends, they pose a significant challenge to forecasting future crime rates. Forecasting has all but disappeared from criminology, in no small part because of embarrassingly erroneous claims of an impending crime boom by a few prominent criminologists just as crime rates were beginning their historic decline in the 1990s. Section 9 contends that, when carefully done, crime forecasting can benefit both policymaking and theory testing and is a natural and needed extension of macrolevel research on crime. The final section of the Element points to improvements in theory, data, and research methods that portend a bright future for the study of crime trends.

This Element is written in nontechnical language and statistics are kept to a minimum. Where statistical terms and procedures are used, they are described in plain language in the text. Interested readers are directed to an appendix for supporting technical material on crime forecasting in Section 9. Much of the story is told in time-series graphs of crime rates and related phenomena (e.g., the age composition of the population, firearm prevalence, inflation, imprisonment, confidence in the police). The story begins in the following section with a description of the major sources of data on crime trends.

## 2 Crime Trends Data

As with anything else worth counting, an accurate description and valid explanations of crime trends require sound data and reliable measurement. This section describes the major data sources used in the study of crime trends.

### 2.1 Uniform Crime Reports

The nation's major source of crime data is the Uniform Crime Reports (UCR). The UCR program began in 1930 and is housed at the FBI.[2] The data consist of eight major violent and property offenses and are based on crimes reported to and recorded by local law enforcement agencies. The violent crimes are criminal homicide, rape, robbery, and aggravated assault and the property crimes are burglary, larceny, motor vehicle theft, and arson. Other generally less serious crimes such as forgery, drug law violations, and simple assaults are also included in the FBI's annual series *Crime in the United States*.

In 2021 the FBI transitioned from the UCR summary system to the National Incident-Based Reporting System (NIBRS), a far more detailed compilation of crime data that is based on individual crime incidents. Many agencies did not report NIBRS data for 2021, however, and the FBI did not include the 2021 data

---

[2] For a brief history of the UCR program, see https://ucr.fbi.gov/crime-in-the-u.s/2010/crime-in-the-u.s.-2010/aboutucrmain.

in its multiyear trend presentations (https://crime-data-explorer.fr.cloud.gov/pages/explorer/crime/crime-trend). The problematic transition to NIBRS reveals a deeper problem in the nation's crime statistics based on law enforcement data: participation in the system is voluntary.

## 2.2 The NIBRS Transition

The FBI released its annual report on crime in the United States for the year 2021 on October 5, 2022. This was the first report under NIBRS, a new and far more detailed data format. NIBRS replaced the UCR "summary system" the FBI has used since the 1930s that includes major felony offenses and arrests recorded by local law enforcement agencies. NIBRS counts many more offenses and provides much greater detail about them, such as the age, sex, and race of victims and the circumstances of the crimes. NIBRS had been in the works since the 1980s, and so full conversion, even if it took nearly forty years to accomplish, has to be counted as good news.

The bad news is that the conversion to NIBRS was far from complete. Only 63% of law enforcement agencies, covering about 65% of the US population, had made the switch to NIBRS by the FBI's deadline of January 1, 2022. And many other agencies submitted NIBRS data that covered only part of the year – just 52% submitted data for all twelve months of 2021. The police departments of some of the nation's largest cities submitted no data at all, including the departments in New York, Los Angeles, Phoenix, and San Francisco. And some states were barely covered by the NIBRS data. Only 15 of California's 740 law enforcement agencies, 40 of Pennsylvania's 1,504 agencies, and 2 of Florida's 757 law enforcement agencies sent in data. The crime data for nonparticipating agencies had to be estimated based on data for prior years and comparisons with agencies of similar population size and composition.

With participation rates this low and uneven, and the need to estimate such a large number of unknowns, the FBI itself cautioned against comparing the 2021 data with data from previous years.[3] That meant that the nation's official crime statistics could not answer the most basic question about crime, whether it is going up or down. That would be a problem in any year. It was an especially serious problem in 2022, when crime had again moved to the forefront of public concerns and loomed as a leading issue in the fall midterm elections. The uncertainties surrounding the crime data were grist for the political mill. If your position is that crime increases are exaggerated, just cite the FBI's estimate

---

[3] The FBI noted: "Due to the full transition to NIBRS and the lack of data for agencies that are not fully transitioned, the 2021 data year cannot be added to the 5-, 10- or 20-year trend presentations that are based in traditional methodologies used with summary data" (https://cde.ucr.cjis.gov/LATEST/webapp/#/pages/explorer/crime/crime-trend).

that robbery went down by 9%. If you want voters to believe crime is out of control, cite the estimate that murder went up over 4%. Either way, who's to say you're right or wrong?

It did not have to be this way. The FBI should not be faulted for pushing hard on NIBRS. It is a much better statistical system and should have been fully implemented long before 2022. Moreover, law enforcement agencies were not caught unawares that NIBRS was coming. The Department of Justice announced the conversion to NIBRS in 2015 and distributed over $120 million to prepare for the transition.[4] But the FBI knew well ahead of the January 2022 deadline that NIBRS participation would be much lower than the 85–95% participation rate in the former summary system and would therefore require far more estimation than needed in the past.[5] At that point, in the fall of 2021, the FBI could have decided to allow agencies that would not be able to meet the upcoming deadline to submit summary data in lieu of NIBRS. The FBI chose instead to require full compliance with NIBRS by the deadline with no exceptions.

The FBI knew that the NIBRS conversion would be a technical challenge for many agencies. That is why they were given fair warning years ago and funds to support the transition. But technical issues were not the primary stumbling block that slowed the transition. The major obstacle was that law enforcement agencies are not required to submit crime data to the FBI. Voluntary participation in the nation's crime reporting system might have made sense in 1930 when the FBI's Uniform Crime Reporting Program was established. Many law enforcement agencies, with venerable traditions of independence and local control, would have resisted a mandate to send sensitive information to Washington that would be made public and could be used to criticize their performance. But the days when crime data were treated as the personal property of the local sheriff or police chief are long gone. If the FBI cannot or will not require local law enforcement to submit their crime data, Congress can, and should.

A federal mandate to submit crime data to the FBI would not have guaranteed full participation in NIBRS, but it probably would have increased participation, reducing the need for extensive estimation. Meanwhile, the FBI put itself in the odd position of mandating that local agencies submit crime data under the NIBRS system while not requiring that they submit any crime data at all.[6] We are left with the hope that 2021 was a one-off anomaly in the nation's ninety-year-old crime

---

[4]  See www.justice.gov/opa/blog/new-and-better-crime-data-nation.

[5]  See www.fbi.gov/news/stories/five-things-to-know-about-nibrs-112520.

[6]  Forty-nine states submit their crime data to a state UCR program, which does some quality control before sending the data on to the FBI. Some of these states require that local law enforcement agencies submit their data to the state, although the degree to which such mandates are enforced is unclear.

data infrastructure. A serious glitch to be sure, and one that could have been avoided, but a teachable moment that offers important lessons for how to operate a bona fide federal statistical system.

## 2.3 National Crime Victimization Survey

A strength of the UCR-NIBRS data is that they are available for counties, cities, metropolitan areas, and census regions as well as the nation as a whole. The data are subject to crime classification errors, however, and the county-level data are often incomplete (Maltz and Targonski 2002; Nolan et al. 2011). The chief drawback of the UCR data, however, is that they exclude crimes that are not reported to the police.

The second major source of US crime data and statistics is the National Crime Victimization Survey (NCVS). The NCVS is an annual survey since 1973 of the US household population that asks whether individuals age twelve and older have been the victim of a property crime or violent crime, excluding homicide, during the last six months. Respondents are also asked whether the crime was reported to the police. The extent of unreported crimes varies substantially across offense types. For example, in 2019 victims or others reported 79.5% of motor vehicle thefts to the police, compared with just 33.9% of rapes or other sexual assaults (Morgan and Thompson 2021).

NCVS data are currently available for the nation as a whole and a subset of states (Kena and Morgan 2023). One limitation is that persons who reside in institutional settings such as jails or nursing homes are not included in the survey. The NCVS does provide a more complete picture of crime than the UCR, however, and the two crime data systems should be viewed as complementing one another, with one filling in the gaps left by the other (Lynch and Addington 2007; Morgan and Thompson 2022).

## 2.4 Other Homicide Data Sources

Three additional US data sources are available for homicide. One is the FBI's Supplementary Homicide Reports (SHR), which provides data on homicide incidents by victim and offender (when known) age, race, and sex; weapon type; victim–offender relationship (e.g., family member, intimate partner, acquaintance, stranger); and attributes of the incident (e.g., drug-related, gang-related, argument). A second source is the Fatal Injury Reports from the National Vital Statistics System (NVSS), which compiles homicide and other data on cause of death from local coroners and medical examiners. Homicide counts and rates are typically somewhat higher than those from the UCR and SHR, in part because reporting to the NVSS is mandatory while reporting to the UCR is voluntary. Nonetheless, time trends derived from the two homicide data sources correspond closely (see https://bjs.ojp.gov/content/pub/pdf/ntmh.pdf). The National Violent Death Reporting System (NVDRS), begun in 2002, compiles data on violent deaths from multiple sources and has been implemented in all fifty states, the District of Columbia, and Puerto Rico.

## 2.5 Nongovernmental and European Sources

Other nongovernmental crime data sources are also available for particular jurisdictions, offense types, and time periods in the United States. For example, the Gun Violence Archive compiles data from multiple sources on gun-related homicides, suicides, and injuries. The Council on Criminal Justice publishes monthly trend data from the police departments of several dozen large cities for ten different offenses. AH Datalytics provides year-to-date homicide data from the police departments of about eighty large cities.

In addition to US sources, data sources for international crime data include the European Sourcebook of Crime and Criminal Justice Statistics, the International Crime Victimization Survey (see Van Dijk et al. 2022), the United Nations Surveys on Crime Trends and the Operations of Criminal Justice Systems, and, for homicide, the World Health Organization. Descriptions and data bases for these and the US sources are listed in Appendix I.

Criminology does not suffer from a lack of data to track crime trends in the United States and elsewhere, although each source contains strengths and limitations that should always be examined and compared with those of other sources. Moreover, it should be kept in mind that, with the exception of the SHR, all of the crime data sources used in this Element are limited to counts and rates of criminal *victimization* and not offending. Even the SHR data on homicide offenders must be viewed with caution because of the large amount of missing data, which has prompted researchers to impute estimates for the unobserved offender attributes (Fox and Swatt 2009). Finally, as discussed in the final section, crime trends may differ in important ways across areas within cities, and the data needed to track these subunit trends are not available in standardized form. With these caveats in mind, we now turn to how the crime data have been used to develop and test hypotheses on the sources of change in crime rates over time.

## 3 The Impact on Violent Crime of Property Crime, Guns, and Prisons

The study of US crime trends has its share of contentious issues. Three of them are addressed in this section. The first may not seem at all controversial: Are trends in homicide and property crime related to one another? If so, is property

crime a *cause* of violent crime? In a prominent statement, two leading criminologists have responded with a resounding no to the latter question. They
countered that, when it comes to homicide, "crime is not the problem"
(Zimring and Hawkins 1997). With few exceptions this contention seems to
have been taken for granted, or at least has not been critically examined, by
other criminologists. It is subjected to scrutiny here.

The second two issues are highly controversial both inside and outside of
criminology. Does the greater availability of firearms increase or decrease the
homicide rate? The best answer, it turns out, is that firearm prevalence is both
a cause and effect of change over time in homicide. Do increases in imprisonment reduce violent crime? The answer appears to be a qualified yes, but there
are so many caveats it is not likely to calm passions on either side of the heated
debate over incarceration policy. We begin by looking at the connection
between homicide and property crime.

## 3.1 Are Homicide and Property Crime Causally Related?

Throughout the Element data from multiple sources are presented to illustrate
trends in crime and other conditions. As a starting point consider the relationship between trends in homicide and property crime in the United States.
Figure 1 displays UCR homicide and property crime rates per 100,000 US
population between 1960 and 2020. Because the property crime rate is so much
higher than the homicide rate, to reveal the relationship between them over time
they have been scaled on different axes, with property crime on the left and
homicide on the right. Both homicide and property crime increased from 1960
to 1980, fell for a few years, increased again through the early 1990s, and then
dropped more or less continuously for the next two and a half decades during
what has been called the "Great American Crime Decline" (Zimring 2007). Up
until that point, property crime and homicide rates moved together over time.
Almost without fail, whenever property crime increased or decreased, so did
homicide. The correlation between the two series over the sixty-year period is
an impressive .864.[7]

The strong correspondence between the homicide and property crime trends
was interrupted in 2015, when the homicide rate began to rise while the
property crime rate continued to fall. The homicide rate in 2016 was 21%
higher than in 2014. Homicide subsided during the next few years, only to
shoot up again in 2020, this time by 30% over the rate in 2019. Such abrupt and
substantial increases in homicide are unlikely to have been caused by typically

---

[7] A correlation of zero indicates that two variables are unrelated to one another. A correlation of
   1.00 indicates that they are perfectly related.

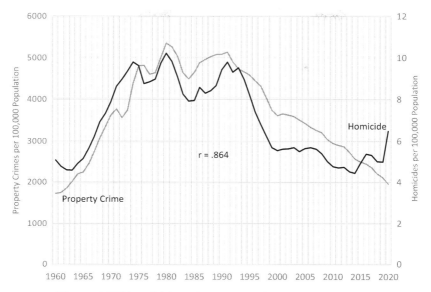

**Figure 1** US homicide and property crime rate, 1960–2020.

**Source:** Uniform Crime Reports

slow-moving changes in demographic and economic conditions. They coincided with widespread social unrest following controversial incidents of police violence in Ferguson, Missouri, in late 2014 and Minneapolis in May 2020. The homicide spike in 2020 also occurred during the first wave of the Covid-19 pandemic. These conditions constituted "exogenous shocks" that altered the normal trajectory of homicide (Rosenfeld 2018). This issue is taken up in Section 8.

The relationship between homicide and property crime trends, at least until the break in 2015, raises the question of whether they are causally related. If we accept the answer by Zimring and Hawkins (1997) that "crime is not the problem" then the apparent relationship between changes over time in homicide and property crime is probably spurious. The sheer magnitude of the long-run relationship, however, and the fact that the year-to-year changes are generally similar[8] suggest that a causal association between homicide and property crime should not be discounted without further investigation.

---

[8] The correlation between the homicide and property crime series in first differences is r=.532. A "first difference" is the difference between the current period's value on a variable and the value for the period before. For example, if this year's homicide rate is six per 100,000 and last year's rate was five, the first difference equals one.

Involvement in property crime exposes offenders to dangerous persons and situations and is a risk factor for violence. Criminal activity typically occurs during the evening hours, away from the home, and in the company of like-minded others, especially among youthful offenders. These activity patterns and associated proximity to offenders raise the probability of violent victimization (Hindelang et al. 1978). Violent crime may result directly from property crime, as when a burglar assaults a homeowner who interrupts his plans. Co-offenders assault and rob one another; criminals sometimes attack or intimidate witnesses, suspected "snitches," or others with incriminating information. In these and other ways, violent crime "feeds off" property crime (Felson 2002: 105–119). Dobrin (2001) found that individuals who have been arrested for property crimes are significantly more likely than others to become the victim of a homicide, controlling for age, race, sex, and local socioeconomic conditions.

Moreover, the huge difference between the volume of property crimes and homicides means that it takes a very small proportion of property crimes to generate a sizable proportion of homicides. In 2019, for example, there were 16,425 homicides and 6,925,677 property crimes recorded by the UCR in the United States, a ratio of 422 property crimes for every homicide. If just one tenth of 1% of the property crimes ended in a homicide, that would generate nearly 7,000 homicides, or about 42% of the total number of homicides in 2019. Property crime does not have to be very violent in the aggregate, therefore, to produce a notable increase in the homicide rate.

## 3.2 Firearms and Homicide

Exposure to other offenders armed with a gun is one way involvement in property crime can contribute to homicide. A controversial issue in criminology is the impact of firearms on the homicide rate. Some analysts claim that an armed society is a safer society. As Lott (1998, 2010) put it, more guns result in less crime. Lott argued that "right to carry" gun laws that expand access to firearms reduce violent crime by making offenders think twice about attacking persons who could be armed. Lott's research has been heavily criticized. A study commissioned by the National Research Council reviewed the available research on the impact of gun laws on violent crime, conducted its own analysis, and concluded that "with the current evidence it is not possible to determine that there is a causal link between the passage of right-to-carry laws and crime rates" (National Research Council 2005: 150).[9] This conclusion was controversial even within the committee itself. One member dissented, arguing

---

[9] I was a member of this NRC committee and endorsed the committee's conclusions and recommendations.

that "the evidence presented by Lott and his supporters suggests that RTC laws do in fact help drive down the murder rate, though their effect on other crimes is ambiguous" (271).

The research on the relationship between the prevalence of firearms and the homicide rate indicates that the relationship is probably reciprocal. Increases in firearm availability spur increases in homicide, and increases in homicide lead to an upswing in firearm acquisition (RAND 2018). There is no disputing that firearms are plentiful in the United States and that the use of a firearm elevates the fatality rate in assaults (Braga et al. 2021; Kleck and McElrath 1991). A key methodological question in research on the relationship between firearm prevalence and homicide is how to measure firearm prevalence. Most of the studies reviewed in RAND (2018) rely on a proxy measure known as "Cook's Index," the percentage of suicides committed with a firearm. This measure has been validated in comparisons with more direct measures of firearm prevalence from surveys (Azrael et al. 2004; but see National Research Council 2005). Figure 2 displays the year-over-year percentage change in the US homicide rate and Cook's Index between 1982 and 2020. The two series are modestly correlated (r=.334), such that increases in firearm prevalence as proxied by the percentage of suicides by firearm tend to be associated with increases in homicide rates. But the correlation between gun prevalence and homicide does not settle debate over whether more guns lead to more homicides or more homicides lead to more guns.

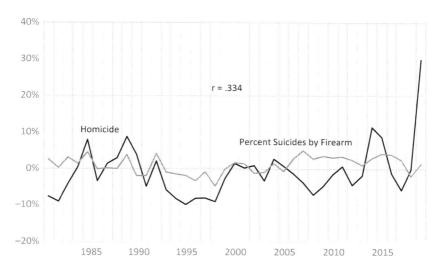

**Figure 2** Year-over-year percentage change in US homicide rate and percentage of suicides committed with a firearm, 1982–2020.

**Source:** Uniform Crime Reports; National Center for Injury Prevention and Control

Efforts to identify the causal direction in the firearms-homicide relationship and, by extension, the precise role of firearm prevalence in the study of homicide trends remain inconclusive (RAND 2018).

## 3.3 Crime and Imprisonment

Another controversial issue in criminology and more broadly is whether imprisonment reduces crime rates and, if so, by how much. For most of the twentieth century, US imprisonment rates were on par with those in most of the developed world, about 100 prisoners per 100,000 population. That began to change in the mid-1970s, when the US prison population started a 30-year rise, peaking at about 500 prisoners per 100,000 population in 2008 and then falling to under 400 per 100,000 in 2020. The past half century has come to be known as the era of "mass incarceration" in the United States.

The logic behind an imprisonment-crime connection is based on assumptions about the deterrent effects and incapacitation effects of imprisonment. In theory, the experience of imprisonment could reduce future offending by deterring former prisoners from committing new crimes (specific deterrence). The threat of imprisonment could reduce crime by deterring the general population from committing crime (general deterrence). Imprisonment could also reduce crime by preventing incarcerated persons from committing crimes against the general public (incapacitation). In practice, it has proven virtually impossible to reliably isolate each of these hypothesized crime-reduction mechanisms from the others in research on the impact of imprisonment on crime rates.

A research review by the National Research Council (2014) concluded that increases in imprisonment rates over time have a modest effect, at best, on crime rates. This conclusion is illustrated in Figure 3, which presents the year-over-year percentage change in the US violent crime rate and imprisonment rate (the number of state and federal prisoners per 100,000) between 1961 and 2020. A small negative[10] correlation exists between the two series (r=-.179), and they frequently move in the same direction, such as during the 1990s crime drop. Most studies report a negative effect of imprisonment on crime – more imprisonment, less crime – although estimates of the magnitude of the imprisonment effect vary so widely that the National Research Council was unable to arrive at a common estimate.

Part of the uncertainty over the impact of imprisonment on crime stems from the fact that the rate of imprisonment is endogenous – that is, it depends on the

---

[10] A "positive" relationship between two variables exists when they both vary in the same direction (i.e., both increase or decrease together). A "negative" relationship means that they vary in opposite directions (i.e., one increases while the other decreases).

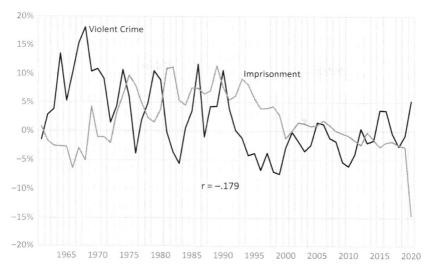

**Figure 3** Year-over-year percentage change in US violent crime rate and imprisonment rate, 1961–2020.

**Source:** Uniform Crime Reports; Bureau of Justice Statistics

crime rate. Other things equal, when the crime rate goes up, so does the imprisonment rate. The relatively few studies that have sought to untangle the mutual causation inherent in the imprisonment–crime relationship find somewhat stronger imprisonment effects on crime than studies that do not adjust the estimates for endogeneity (e.g., Levitt 1996). A second difficulty in precisely determining the effect of changes in the imprisonment rate on changes in the crime rate is that the effect is not constant over the scale of imprisonment: As the imprisonment rate rises, its effect on the crime rate becomes smaller (Johnson and Raphael 2012). Perhaps the best one can say about the effect of the imprisonment rate on the crime rate is that it probably exists, it is probably negative, and its magnitude probably diminishes at higher rates of imprisonment.

## 4 Different Levels, Common Trends: Crime, Race-Ethnicity, and Gender

Group differences in crime rates have long interested criminologists. This section explores differences in crime over time in the United States by race, ethnicity (Hispanic, non-Hispanic), and gender. The section begins by presenting group-specific trends in homicide and then reviews prior research that seeks to explain group similarities and differences in homicide. A key question throughout is whether Black, White, Hispanic, male, and female homicide rates are related to the same or different demographic and socioeconomic explanatory conditions over time.

Studies of crime levels and trends generally focus on homicide, and most study designs are cross-sectional rather than longitudinal. Cross-sectional studies compare places or populations to one another at the same point in time. Longitudinal studies examine places or populations over time. Prior studies have found elevated homicide rates in US cities, counties, and states with high levels of economic deprivation and population density (Land et al. 1990; McCall et al. 2010; Messner and Rosenfeld 1999). US homicide rates have also been linked to the age structure of the population, with homicide victimization and offending disproportionately concentrated among young adults (Phillips 2006). Higher homicide rates have been found in the Southern and Western regions of the country (Lee et al. 2007; O'Carroll and Mercy 1989) and areas where divorce rates are higher (Breault and Kposowa 1997). Other studies have disclosed associations between homicide rates and property crime (Rosenfeld 2009) and the prevalence of firearms (Duggan 2001; Hepburn and Hemenway 2004), although the causal direction of that relationship remains uncertain (RAND 2018).

Homicide rates have been linked to alcohol use and availability (Parker 1995; Parker and Auerhahn 1998) and are also elevated in and around illicit drug markets. Violence is a potent enforcement mechanism when disputes arise over price, purity, and other terms of trade in such "stateless" social spaces (Reuter 2009). Youth firearm violence rose substantially during the crack cocaine epidemic of the late 1980s and early 1990s (Blumstein 1995; Cook and Laub 1998). Recent research has linked higher homicide rates and trends in the non-Latino Black and White populations, but not the Latino population, to the opioid epidemic (Gaston et al. 2019; Rosenfeld et al. 2021a; Rosenfeld et al. 2021b).

## 4.1 Black, White, and Hispanic Homicide Trends

It is widely recognized that homicide rates are higher in the Black population than in the White population in the United States. Less commonly understood is that it has not always been this way. Prior to the twentieth century, White homicide rates often exceeded those in the Black population. Black rates began to rise with increasing urbanization and Jim Crow discrimination at the turn of the century (DuBois 1996[1899]; Roth 2009). The racial gap in homicide rates has varied somewhat in recent decades, but it remains an enduring form of social inequality in the United States.

Figure 4 displays NVSS homicide rates by race and ethnicity between 1990 and 2020. The homicide series begin in 1990 because that is the first year the

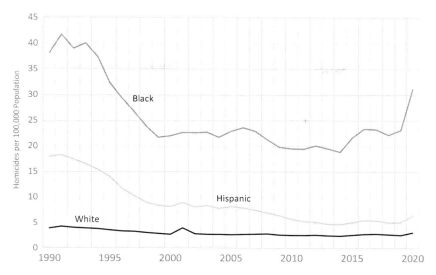

**Figure 4** Non-Hispanic White, non-Hispanic Black, and Hispanic homicide rate, 1990–2020.

**Source:** National Vital Statistics System

NVSS partitioned homicide rates by Hispanic ethnicity. The main takeaway from Figure 4 is the marked difference in homicide *levels* across the three groups over the entire thirty-year period. The non-Hispanic Black homicide rate was roughly ten times greater than the non-Hispanic White rate in the early 1990s. From the late 1990s into the current century the Black–White homicide ratio decreased somewhat before returning to ten-to-one in 2020. Throughout the period Hispanic homicide rates moved between the rates for the non-Hispanic Black and White populations. During the early 1990s, the Hispanic rates were about four times higher than the non-Hispanic White rates. More recently, the Hispanic–White homicide ratio has fallen to about two-to-one.

The large difference in the homicide rates of the three race-ethnic groups shown in Figure 4 makes it difficult to determine whether their year-to-year trends are similar or diverge from one another. Figure 5 places the non-Hispanic Black and White homicide rates on separate vertical axes and reveals very similar patterns of change in the two trends. Both homicide rates fell during the 1990s, flattened during the first years of the current century, rose in 2015 and 2016, and rose again in 2020. Hispanic homicide rates, not shown in Figure 5, follow the same pattern. The only notable divergence between the non-Hispanic Black and White homicide rates occurred in 2001 when White homicides increased as a consequence of the September 11 terrorist attack. The nearly 3,000 deaths from the attack are counted as homicides in the NVSS but not in

*Criminology*

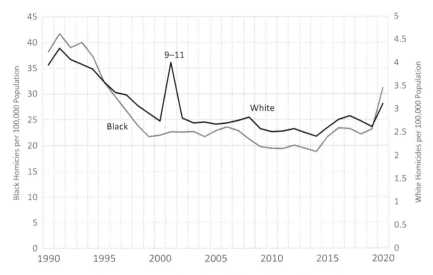

**Figure 5** Non-Hispanic White and non-Hispanic
Black homicide rate, 1990–2020.

**Source:** National Vital Statistics System

the UCR. In general, however, the Black and White homicide series rise and fall together, which suggests that, despite the difference in their levels, their similar time trends result from common causes.

Extensive research has been conducted on the relationship between race and violent crime in the United States. Early studies examined the effect of race, typically percent Black, on total homicide and violent crime rates (e.g., Blau and Blau 1982). More recent research has focused on race-specific rates of homicide and, on occasion, other violent offenses (Steffensmeier et al. 2010). Much of this research has addressed the "racial invariance" thesis, which holds, in general terms, that violence in both the Black and White populations is rooted in the same conditions of structural disadvantage (see Sampson et al. 2018, for a comprehensive review). A few studies have included the Hispanic population in assessments of the invariance thesis (Light and Ulmer 2016; Phillips 2002; Steffensmeier et al. 2010; Ulmer et al. 2012). Other recent research has investigated levels and time trends in the Black–White homicide gap (e.g., LaFree et al. 2010; Light and Ulmer 2016; Lo et al. 2012; Ulmer et al. 2012; Velez et al. 2003).

Results of evaluations of the racial invariance thesis depend on how "invariance" is defined (Steffensmeier et al. 2010). If invariance means that similar conditions of structural disadvantage are significantly associated *in the same direction* with Black and White homicide rates, research results generally support the thesis (Light and Ulmer 2016; Sampson and Wilson 1995; Sampson et al. 2018). But if the invariance thesis also requires that the *magnitude* of the effects of structural disadvantage not differ significantly[11] for Black and White homicide, the research is less supportive (Ousey 1999; Phillips 2002; Steffensmeier et al. 2010). Even the less restrictive conception of invariance has been challenged, for example by research showing that Black and White homicide rates are uncorrelated across metropolitan areas, which implies that the sources of the race-specific rates are different (Feld and Bauldry 2018). A further complication arises from the problem of "restricted distributions," or non-overlapping race-specific measures of structural disadvantage (McNulty 2001; Ulmer et al. 2012). Finally, mixed results regarding the effect of racial segregation on homicide rates is an additional source of uncertainty in research on the invariance thesis.

Sound theoretical reasons exist for positing a positive effect of residential racial segregation on homicide in the Black population. Massey (1995) points out that because segregation concentrates the correlates of violence in Black communities, it also concentrates high rates of violence in these geographic areas. Not all research finds a significant effect of segregation on the racial gap in homicide (e.g., LaFree et al. 2010; Phillips 2002). Studies that do find a segregation effect on Black homicide rates – which is consistently positive – report a null or negative effect on White rates, especially in the context of "hyper" or "macro" segregation that crosses municipal boundaries (Light and Thomas 2019; Massey 1995; O'Flaherty and Sethi 2010; but see Peterson and Krivo 2010). The contrasting effects of racial segregation on Black and White homicide rates could be interpreted as contradicting the racial invariance thesis advanced by Sampson et al. (2018), who argue that if one factor consistently reduces homicide in one community and increases it in another "that would be evidence against the theory" (p. 17).

Though Latinos are the largest ethnic minority in the United States, fewer studies of their crime patterns exist than those of non-Latino Black and White Americans. As shown in Figure 4, nationwide Latino homicide rates are somewhat higher than those in the non-Latino White population and much lower than in the non-Latino Black population. Between 2016 and 2020, the yearly average Latino homicide rate was 5.5 per 100,000 population, the non-Latino White rate was 2.8 per 100,000, and the non-Latino Black rate was 24.7 per 100,000.[12] The research on homicide that includes the Latino

---

[11] A statistically "significant" relationship between two variables is unlikely to be attributable to chance.

[12] The homicide data are from the CDC's Center for Injury Prevention and Control (https://wisqars .cdc.gov/fatal-reports).

population has found that Latino immigration into the United States either is unrelated to or reduces crime and violence and that Latino homicide rates are related to the same conditions of structural disadvantage as the homicide rates in the non-Latino Black and White populations.

There is a strong research consensus that immigration generally and Latino immigration in particular are unrelated to or negatively associated with crime and violence in the United States (see the extensive research review in Ousey and Kubrin 2018). Non-Latino White, non-Latino Black, and Latino homicide rates all are related to levels of poverty, female headship, and other indicators of structural disadvantage (Steffensmeier et al. 2010; Ulmer et al. 2012). Phillips (2002) estimated that about half of the Black–White homicide gap would be eliminated if the Black and White population had the same demographic and socioeconomic characteristics. Over 100% of the homicide gap between non-Latino Whites and Latinos would be eliminated – the homicide rate of the Latino population, in other words, would be *lower* than that of the non-Latino White population – if they experienced identical structural conditions (see Lauritsen et al. 2018, for a similar result with respect to the nonlethal violence gap).

The idea that violent crime in the Latino population is lower than would be expected based on indicators of structural disadvantage has been termed the "Latino paradox" and "immigrant revitalization perspective" (Feldmeyer et al. 2022; Martinez 2002; Martinez and Lee 2000; Sampson 2008; Ulmer et al. 2012). According to this thesis, violence is buffered by chain migration into cohesive immigrant communities with strong family bonds and comparatively high levels of economic and social capital. The bulk of the research supporting this perspective, however, is based on one or a few traditional Latino migration destinations situated along the Mexican border. Whether emerging Latino settlement areas away from the border offer the same protections against violence remains an open question (Harris and Feldmeyer 2013).

The diffusion of Latino immigrants from traditional settlement areas to non-traditional destinations further inland has been described as "perhaps the most significant trend in U.S. population redistribution over the past quarter century" (Lichter and Johnson 2009: 497). Immigrant growth rates in the newer destinations in the Midwest and South are three to five times greater than in the traditional settlement areas of the Southwest (Lichter and Johnson 2009). Both push and pull factors have fueled growth in these newer settlement areas: economic stagnation in traditional settlement areas of the Southwest and greater economic opportunities in the newer ones (Ludwig-Dehm and Iceland 2017). Another possible push factor is stricter enforcement of immigration laws and border patrol scrutiny in the traditional destinations (Harris and Feldmeyer 2013).

Traditional and emerging Latino migration destinations differ in ways that are potentially relevant to the study of crime trends. Education levels are higher and the degree of concentrated poverty among Latinos is lower in nontraditional areas (Lichter and Johnson 2009; Ludwig-Dehm and Iceland 2017). These and other differences have prompted empirical examinations of violent crime in traditional and emerging Latino settlement areas directed at the question of whether the protective effects of strong community and family bonds found in the traditional locales extend to the newer migration destinations. The results of this research are mixed. Cross-sectional investigations generally find that protection against violent crime is greater in traditional settlement areas (e.g., Feldmeyer et al. 2022; Shihadeh and Barranco 2010; Xie and Baumer 2018), whereas a recent longitudinal study finds a negative relationship or no relationship between immigration and Latino, non-Latino Black, and non-Latino White homicide rates in both traditional and newer settlement areas (Light 2017).

In summary, extensive prior research has found that the same conditions of structural disadvantage affect both non-Latino Black and White homicide rates, although the magnitude of the effects may differ. An exception is racial segregation, which elevates Black homicide and reduces or is unrelated to White homicide. More limited research has disclosed significant effects of structural disadvantage and significant or null effects of immigration on Latino homicide. Poverty and family disruption tend to increase Latino homicide rates and immigration is unrelated to or reduces them. The terms "elevates," "increase" and "reduces" are used advisedly because most of the relevant research is cross-sectional and does not reveal movement in homicide and other conditions over time. That said, the research literature tends to favor the idea that the common trends in race and ethnic homicide rates are related to common causes.

## 4.2 Male and Female Homicide Trends

A simple, if exaggerated, way of summarizing gender patterns in homicide is that men kill men, women kill men, and men kill women. There is no disputing that men do most of the killing and are killed the most in nearly every society for which we have records. But are changes over time in male and female homicide victimization rates similar or different?

Figure 6 displays male and female homicide trends from 1981 to 2020. Because the male rates are several times higher than the female rates, the two series are scaled on separate axes.

The male and female trends closely track one another. They rise and fall together in a pattern that resembles the overall homicide trend shown in Figure 1. As with the race-ethnic trends it appears that many of the same underlying conditions may

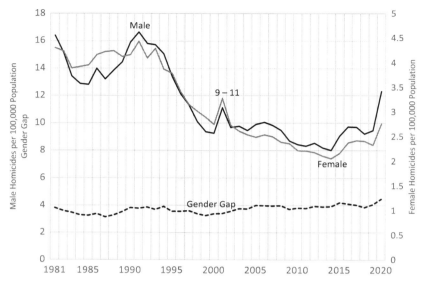

**Figure 6** Male and female homicide rate, 1981–2020.
**Source:** National Vital Statistics System

help to explain the parallel trajectories of male and female homicide. Recent research has identified some of the explanatory factors related to trends in homicide and nonfatal violence among males and females in the United States.

### 4.2.1 The Gender Gap in Violence and Women's Emancipation

During the 1970s criminologists Freda Adler (1975) and Rita Simon (1975) advanced an intriguing and controversial argument tying escalating female crime rates to transformations in women's status and roles. They contended that, just as the gender gap in economic opportunities and involvement in public life had narrowed, so too had the gender gap in criminal behavior. This claim, which became known as the "liberation hypothesis," struck many observers at the time as quite plausible. As women came to resemble men in their legitimate circumstances and activities, with their associated pressures and inducements, why wouldn't women's crime rates become more like men's as well?

No sooner had the liberation hypothesis been launched, however, it attracted criticism from other criminologists. Some analysts questioned whether the gender gap in crime, particularly in violence, had in fact narrowed over time (e.g., Steffensmeier 1980). Others agreed that the gender gap in violence has narrowed and that women's social and economic advancement is an important reason why, but disputed the one-sided assumption that women have become more like men in their criminal behavior. Why, they asked, is it not just as reasonable to assume that women's emancipation has made men more like women (Rosenfeld 2000)?

This idea is rooted in Norbert Elias's (1978 [1939]) "civilizing hypothesis" on declining levels of violence over several centuries (see Pinker 2012, for a popular account). According to Elias, growing interdependencies in social relations over time, evolving cultural sensibilities that define displays of aggressive behavior as uncouth and "animalistic," and the modern state's monopolization of the means of violence increased self-restraint and reduced tolerance for interpersonal violence. Elias was explicit about the role women played in the civilizing process: "Social opinion is determined to a high degree by women. It remains to be shown in more detail how decisive this first wave of emancipation of women was for the civilizing process, for the advance of the frontier of shame and embarrassment and for the strengthening of social control over the individual" (quoted in Lauritsen et al. 2022). Pinker (2012) picked up on this idea and maintained that social settings that include women are more peaceful than all-male settings because women have little tolerance for male dominance displays. Borrowing from the routine activity perspective in criminology, Lauritsen et al. (2022) added that women may act as "capable guardians" in situations in which men might otherwise act out violently. In short, these researchers argued, men behave less violently when women are around.

Lauritsen et al. (2022) offered the civilizing process as one of several hypotheses to explain the declining gender gap in violence. Contrary to the liberation thesis, they pointed out that the gender gap has narrowed during the past several decades, not because women's rate of violence has increased but because male violence has decreased more than female violence (Lauritsen and Heimer 2008; Lauritsen et al. 2009). The gender gap has decreased in violent victimization to the point that female and male rates of serious violent victimization – the sum of sexual assault and rape, aggravated assault, and robbery – are now essentially equal (Lauritsen et al. 2022). The gender gap in violent offending has also narrowed, but male offending rates still exceed those among females (Lauritsen et al. 2009). Two exceptions are the gender gap in homicide victimization, which has changed little over time, as shown in Figure 6, and in intimate partner violence, discussed herein. While nonfatal violence has decreased among both men and women, the outstanding question is why, with the exceptions noted, the decline has been greater among men. These researchers suggest that something like the civilizing process, especially women's greater involvement in public life, may hold a clue.

In a study of NCVS data on trends in violent victimization between 1973 and 2015, Lauritsen et al. (2022) found that the gender gap in violent victimization is significantly associated with women's labor force participation rate, which they argue is a good measure of women's presence in public life. As women's participation in the labor force increased over time, the gender gap in violence decreased. Increasing female labor force participation, in other words, contributed to a greater decline in male than in female violent victimization. The researchers were quick to point out that other factors not included in their analysis could also have led to a decline in the gender gap in violence. But their study, which is based on millions of interviews and includes multiple controls for respondents' age, race, employment status, and other individual attributes, offers compelling initial evidence for the idea, put simply, that women's greater participation in public life has helped to pacify men.

### 4.2.2 Intimate Partner Violence

Criminologists and other researchers have devoted substantial attention to trends in violence among intimate partners (i.e., married, separated, divorced, never married couples). The research results differ depending on whether the focus is on fatal or nonfatal violence.

### Homicide

Studies of intimate partner homicide trends have uncovered two robust facts about this type of killing: (1) Women's victimization rates are several times higher than men's, and (2) men's victimization rates have declined more than women's over time (Browne and Williams 1993; Browne et al. 1999; Fridel and Fox 2019; Puzone et al. 2000). The first fact is not surprising. Victims' advocates have effectively defined domestic violence as violence against women.[13] The second fact, at first glance, is more puzzling. Given the widespread public attention to and growth in protective services and resources for female victims of intimate partner violence, how can we explain the greater decline in *male* victimization rates? Part of the answer appears to be that the increasing availability of assistance for female victims of intimate partner violence has helped to save men's lives.

Researchers have relied on two key concepts to explain this seeming paradox in intimate partner homicide trends: *victim precipitation* and *exposure reduction*. A sizable number of homicides in general, and most intimate partner homicides committed by women, are precipitated by the victim (Campbell et al. 2007; Wolfgang 1958). Women kill in these situations to stop violence or abuse by their partners or ex-partners. It follows that interventions that reduce

---

[13] See, for example, UN Committee on the Elimination of Discrimination Against Women (CEDAW), CEDAW General Recommendation No. 19: Violence against women, 1992, www .refworld.org/docid/52d920c54.html.

their exposure to violent intimates may obviate the need, put bluntly, to kill their way out of the relationship.

One such mechanism of exposure reduction is the liberalization of divorce laws. When access to divorce is made easier for women and "unilateral" (i.e., one spouse can initiate the divorce without the consent of the other), spousal homicide, especially against men, should decline. Consistent with this hypothesis, studies have linked decreasing rates of male victimization in spousal homicide to rising divorce rates (Dugan et al. 1999; Rosenfeld 1997). Some research has found that unilateral divorce also reduces nonfatal spousal violence (Stevenson and Wolfers 2006).

Another means of exposure reduction is to provide assistance in the form of domestic violence hotlines, shelters, and legal aid to women, and often their children, to facilitate exiting violent or abusive relationships. Here again, the research is supportive. Studies have shown greater declines in male intimate partner homicide rates in cities and states where such domestic violence resources are more plentiful (Browne and Williams 1989; Dugan et al. 1999). In a subsequent study, Dugan et al. (2003) found an exception that, in effect, proves the rule of exposure reduction. Not all kinds of domestic violence resources, they discovered, necessarily reduce intimate partner homicide. Some in fact may increase it "suggesting a retaliation effect when interventions stimulate increased aggression without adequately reducing exposure" (169).

## Nonfatal Violence

Trends in nonfatal intimate partner violence are not as easily summarized or explained as the homicide trends. Figure 7, from Lauritsen et al. (2022), displays trends in rates of nonfatal serious violence victimization (sexual assault and rape, aggravated assault, and robbery) among male and female intimate partners based on NCVS data from 1973 to 2020.[14] We see that, like the gender difference in levels of intimate partner homicide, rates of nonfatal intimate partner violence are much higher among females than males. The female and male rates both rose from the early 1970s through the early 1990s and then declined through the beginning of the current century. The gender gap in nonfatal intimate violence (the ratio of the female rate to the male rate) narrowed when the female and male rates were rising, because the increase in the male rates was greater than the increase in the female rates. It continued to narrow when both rates were falling, because the decrease in the female rates exceeded the decrease in the male rates. The female rates remained essentially flat during the first two decades of the current century,

---

[14] In 1980 the NCVS expanded the definition of intimate partner violence to include boyfriend and girlfriend and ex-boyfriend and ex-girlfriend.

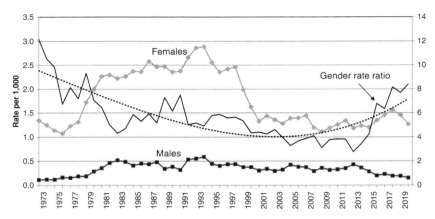

**Figure 7** Gender gap in serious violence by intimate partners: 1973–2020.
**Source:** Lauritsen et al. (2022)

while the male rates decreased from 2014 to 2020, which widened the gender gap in nonfatal intimate violence, returning it to where it was in the late 1970s.

This is a more complicated pattern than we saw in the intimate partner homicide trends. Ideally, both fatal and nonfatal intimate violence should be explained by the same theory. Feminist theories that highlight the role of patriarchy are able to explain gender differences in the *levels* of fatal and nonfatal intimate violent but do not as readily accommodate differences in the *trends*, especially in nonfatal violence. Incorporating movement over time into theories of intimate partner violence is a major task for those committed to explaining and reducing violence against both women and men.

## 5 Crime, Age, and Birth Cohorts

The relationship between crime and age is as close to a "law" as any research finding in criminology. An influential modern statement on the age–crime relationship is from Michael Gottfredson and Travis Hirschi (Gottfredson and Hirschi 1990; Hirschi and Gottfredson 1983). They observed that criminal behavior increases during adolescence and young adulthood and declines thereafter. This developmental sequence, in their view, is not a function of changing social circumstances through the life course. It is simply a consequence of the "inexorable aging of the organism." Not surprisingly, this proposition has sparked considerable criticism and research, although few analysts dispute the correlation between crime and age, even if they believe it is explicable in terms of related changes in social and psychological factors. One empirical assessment, for example, concluded that "the relationship between age and crime in adolescence and early adulthood is largely explainable, though not entirely attributable, to multiple co-occurring developmental changes" (Sweeten et al. 2013: 921).

The age–crime relationship, originally formulated at the individual level, has also been evaluated at the aggregate level of analysis. The aggregate-level application of the age-crime curve is straightforward: If criminal behavior increases in adolescence and young adulthood and decreases thereafter then, all else equal, changes over time in aggregate crime rates should correspond with changes in the proportion of the population in this age cohort. The crime rise during the 1960s and 1970s in the United States has been attributed, in part, to the coming of age of the post–Second World War baby boom cohorts (Sagi and Wellford 1968). Similarly, the aging of the baby boomers into adulthood contributed to the dip in crime rates during the early 1980s (Steffensmeier and Harer 1987).

These trends in crime and the age composition of the population are illustrated in Figure 8, which depicts changes between 1960 and 2020 in the US homicide rate and the percentage of the population between the ages of fifteen and twenty-nine.[15]

We see that both climbed from the mid-1960s to a peak in 1980 and then fell during the following five years. But it is also evident from the

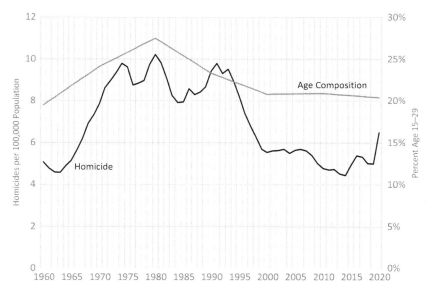

**Figure 8** US homicide rate and age composition, 1960–2020.
**Source:** Uniform Crime Reports; US Census Bureau

---

[15] Percent 15–29 interpolated between census years.

figure that the relationship between homicide and age composition, as measured by the adolescent and young adult segment of the population, is far from perfect.

The homicide rate rose during the late 1980s and early 1990s, the period of the crack epidemic, as the relative size of the 15- to 29-year-old age cohort continued to shrink. After 2000, the size of the youthful cohort was basically flat, while the homicide rate both decreased and increased. Clearly, other things are not always equal with respect to the relationship between trends in the age composition of the population and homicide.

Given the higher rates of crime in the younger age groups, it might be assumed that aggregate crime trends are always and exclusively driven by adolescents and young adults. Recent research, however, suggests that has not always been the case since the 1960s. It is true that the late 1980s homicide rise was almost exclusively the product of homicide increases in the younger age cohorts; homicide rates were flat or fell in the population over the age of thirty (Blumstein and Wallman 2000). But all but the very oldest age groups participated in the homicide boom of the 1960s and 1970s. And the homicide increases in 2015 and 2020 were more evenly distributed by age than was the increase in the late 1980s (Rogers et al. 2023). If anything, the youth homicide boom during the crack cocaine era is more the exception than the rule of changing homicide rates over time.

Most of the aggregate-level longitudinal research on the relationship between age composition and crime has examined age effects on the total crime rate. Some researchers, however, have explored the connection between the size of age cohorts and age-specific crime rates. This line of inquiry has been guided by the "Easterlin hypothesis," which holds that larger younger-age cohorts will have higher crime rates than smaller ones because they weaken social controls and increase economic and social stress (Easterlin 1980). According to Easterlin, the baby boom cohorts experienced crowded classrooms and labor markets and diminished adult supervision as they aged, which in turn led to more crime. Some studies support this hypothesis, while others do not (Steffensmeier et al. 1987). However, the general insight that the relative size of birth cohorts can influence age-specific crime rates is an important foundation for the "age-period-cohort" research of the past generation.

It has long been recognized that crime rates are a function of three basic effects: age effects (a), discussed earlier; period effects (p), the influence of contemporaneous economic, social, and cultural conditions; and cohort effects (c), the influence of the environment into which different population cohorts are born and mature. Research in recent decades has sought to untangle the separate influences of age, period, and cohort on crime trends (e.g., Greenberg and Larkin 1985; Kim et al. 2016; Lu et al. 2022; O'Brien and Stockard 2009). All of this research runs into the same methodological problem: It is not possible, without adjustment, to unravel the separate effects of age, period, and cohort on crime rates, because they are linearly dependent. Any two of the components perfectly determine the third.

A variety of methodological fixes have been used to identify APC models, most of which are reasonable on their face, but no more reasonable than alternatives that produce substantively different results (Spelman 2022). Spelman (2022) offers his own method for solving the APC identification problem, which he acknowledges is unlikely to end debate over the proper solution. His results indicate that period effects were largely responsible for the crime drop of the 1990s and the crime rise preceding it, but that age and cohort effects explain violent and property crime trends since 2000.

Despite their methodological differences, a universal finding of the APC research is that cohort effects matter for explaining crime trends, even if different studies produce different estimates of their magnitude. Yet most research on crime trends, including my own, focuses on co-occurring social and economic conditions and omits consideration of the effects of the circumstances of birth and early childhood on crime in adolescence and young adulthood. A well-known and controversial exception is research on the effect of legalized abortion in the 1970s on the crime drop of the 1990s. Donohue and Levitt (2001, 2020) argued that increased access to abortion reduced the number of unplanned births, resulting in smaller cohorts, improvements in the circumstances of early childhood, and lower crime rates about twenty years later. They estimated that abortion legalization explained as much as 50% of the 1990s crime drop. Another exception is research on the impact of reduced exposure to lead during childhood on criminal behavior later in life, which, according to Reyes (2007), produced a 56% drop in violent crime.

The abortion and lead hypotheses, especially their proponents' outsized claims concerning the impact of a single factor on crime trends, have not stood up well against subsequent research by other scholars (e.g., Joyce 2009; Lauritsen et al. 2016). Yet, these cohort-based studies are notable because they illustrate the importance of the contingencies of birth and early development, whatever they may be, for understanding why crime rates move up and down over time. They also are a reminder that birth cohort effects have received too little attention in crime trends research. As one analyst has concluded: "It is time we returned our attention to what we once knew: Crime rises and falls based on the life experiences and decisions of young children" (Spelman 2022: 665).

## 6 Crime and the Economy

Interest in the relationship between changing economic conditions and crime rates is as old as the study of crime trends itself. With the emergence of industrial capitalist societies and their periodic "boom-bust" economic swings, attention turned to the impact of the business cycle on crime trends. A major early study was by Dorothy Swaine Thomas (1927), who investigated the association between the business cycle and crime rates between 1857 and 1913 in Britain. Thomas found that burglary and robbery rates rose during economic downturns. Other than robbery, however, changing economic conditions had no effect on violent crime rates. A half century later, Cook and Zarkin (1985) reported similar results in a study of crime rates and the business cycle in the United States between 1933 and 1982. Burglary and robbery rates turned up during recessions, which had little to no effect on homicide rates. A replication with twenty-six years of additional data produced similar results (Bushway et al. 2013).

There are two prominent exceptions to the results showing increases in acquisitive crime during economic downturns: the Great Depression of the 1930s and the 2008–2009 Great Recession. Both violent and property crime rates decreased during these devastating economic crashes. Moreover, crime rates rose during the prosperous 1960s, prompting James Q. Wilson to coin the expression "crime amidst plenty" (Wilson 1985). After crime rates decreased during the Great Recession, Wilson (2011) sounded the same theme in an op-ed for the *Wall Street Journal*: Crime is unrelated to economic hardship, and the crime drop resulted from high rates of imprisonment, smart policing strategies, improved home security, and a decline in drug abuse.

In a multicausal world, it is possible that the Great Recession did exert upward pressure on crime rates, but not enough to offset the effects of incarceration, policing, target hardening, or other crime-reducing factors. Or perhaps the Great Depression and Great Recession differed from other economic downturns in ways that blunted crime increases. The latter possibility is explored in this section.

Until recently, the research literature on the relationship between economic conditions and crime trends was puzzling at best and grim at worst.[16] Puzzling because studies consistently returned mixed results; grim because the results could be used to support almost any conclusion about how, or whether, the economy affects crime rates (Bushway 2011; Rosenfeld 2011). Around the turn of the current century, however, the "consensus of doubt" (Chiricos 1987) began

---

[16] This section draws from Rosenfeld and Levin (2016).

to give way to a new research consensus regarding the relationship between the economy and crime.

Several studies confirmed the ages-old belief that worsening economic conditions produce disorder and crime. The new consensus was fueled, in part, by replacement or supplementation of the unemployment rate, the long-standing economic indicator of choice in research on crime trends, with other economic indicators. A good bit of the groundwork for the recent research on the economy and crime was established by Cook and Zarkin (1985), who found that rates of robbery and property crime tend to increase during recessions and decline during recoveries. Arvanites and Defina (2006) found that state-level gross domestic product per capita is significantly related to property crime trends in US states in the expected direction: as output falls, crime rates increase. They found no significant effect of unemployment on property crime. Rosenfeld and Fornango (2007) replicated these results and also found that collective perceptions of economic change, or "consumer sentiment," are significantly associated with acquisitive crime trends. During periods of rising consumer confidence and optimism, acquisitive crime rates fall, and when confidence wanes, crime rates rise. Similar results for the effects of consumer sentiment were reported in a comparative study of burglary rates in the United States and European nations (Rosenfeld and Messner 2009).

Grogger (1998) and Gould et al. (2002) found an inverse relationship between wages and youth crime in the United States, and some studies even showed the expected positive effect of unemployment on acquisitive crime trends (e.g., Raphael and Winter-Ebmer 2001). The new consensus in findings concerning the relationship between economic conditions and acquisitive crime is matched by convergence in results showing little or no relationship with homicide and other violent crimes, except for robbery. One exception is a study by Lauritsen and Heimer (2010), who found significant effects of economic conditions on trends in male serious violence victimization. Another is research on inflation and homicide in US cities, discussed next.

The 2008–2009 recession threatened to reinstate the consensus of doubt concerning the effect of economic conditions on crime (Wilson 2011). Between 2007 and 2009, US unemployment rates more than doubled, real GDP and wages fell, and consumer confidence plummeted. But robbery and property crime rates did not rise; they dropped by 10% and 7%, respectively, over the two years. At the very least, these seemingly anomalous patterns posed a challenge to the new research consensus on crime and the economy. If deteriorating economic conditions drive up crime, how are we to explain falling crime rates during a severe recession?

There is no disputing the gravity of the 2008–2009 recession. By some measures, it was worse than all previous downturns since the Great Depression of the 1930s. Comparisons of the 2008–2009 recession with the Great Depression are often overdrawn. But on one key economic indicator, the two crises were similar: Consumer prices stagnated and fell in both periods. Price deflation was far greater during the first years of the Depression, but in 2009 consumer prices fell for the first time in over fifty years. Although price increases often slow during recessions, they rarely turn negative. That has happened only three times in the twelve officially recorded recessions in the United States since the Great Depression: in 1949, 1954, and 2009.

If the 2008–2009 recession differs from most others in price behavior, what relevance does this have for criminal behavior? A suggestive historical case can be made that changing crime rates coincide with price changes. As prices fell during the 1930s, crime rates did as well. We might then add price deflation to the list of proposed solutions to the riddle of why crime dropped during the Great Depression (see, e.g., Johnson et al. 2007). Both crime and consumer prices were at historic lows during the 1950s. And what of the paradox of "crime amidst plenty" in the 1960s (Wilson 1985)? In fact, prices began a steep rise in the mid-1960s, and crime rates followed suit (see LaFree 1998).

What happens to a society when consumer prices skyrocket? We have vivid historical examples of the havoc that runaway inflation can cause: Germany immediately after the First World War, Argentina during most of the past four decades, Venezuela after the election of President Madoro in 2013. In each instance, mass suffering ensued, political conflict increased, civil disorder spread, and crime rates rose (Rosenfeld and Vogel 2023). While suggestive, these historical parallels offer only impressionistic evidence of the connection between extreme inflation and crime. But more modest price increases can also spark crime and social strife, as was the case in the late 1960s and 1970s when US crime rates rose sharply during a period of sustained inflation.

The relationship between the US property crime rate and inflation between 1960 and 2020 is depicted in Figure 9. Also shown are periods of recession during the sixty-year timespan. In general, as inflation increased from 1960 to 1990, so did property crime. Both inflation and property crime then fell over the next thirty years. (The Pearson's correlation between the two series is r=.624.) We also see that both inflation and property crime rates were elevated during the recessions of the 1970s and 1980s and, to a lesser extent, during the recession in 1990–1991. That was not the case during the recession in 2001, however, nor during the Great Recession of 2008–2009, when inflation turned negative (i.e., prices fell in absolute terms) and property crime continued to decrease.

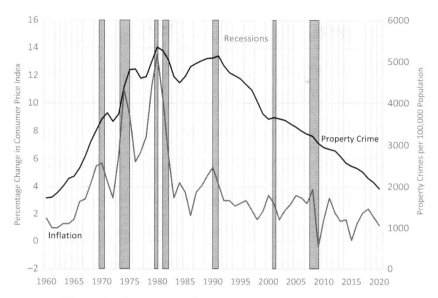

**Figure 9** US property crime rate and inflation, 1960–2020.

**Source:** Uniform Crime Reports; Bureau of Labor Statistics; National Bureau of Economic Research

The differences in the trajectory of property crime during recessions since 1960 are not attributable to economic growth or unemployment; a slowdown in growth rates and an increase in unemployment are defining characteristics of recessions. As Figure 9 suggests, however, the earlier and more recent recessions since 1960 can be distinguished by the behavior of inflation, which rose in the former and moderated or fell in the latter. Recessionary periods, of course, may differ in respects that are unrelated to economic conditions but are related to crime rates. Yet, the forgoing suggests a tentative hypothesis: Whether robbery and property crime rates rise or fall during an economic downturn depends on the change in consumer prices. If inflation accelerates, so will rates of acquisitive crime; if inflation declines, acquisitive crime will as well. Both logic and evidence support this hypothesis.

## 6.1 Crime, Inflation, and Underground Markets

Persons engaged in income-producing crime must have a way of disposing of the goods they steal that they do not consume. They can give them away, sell them for cash, or exchange them for something else of value. Gifts aside, property offenders perforce must become involved in underground or "off-the-books" transactions because it is illegal to buy and sell stolen goods. Applying standard economic theory, the greater the demand for stolen goods, the higher the returns to acquisitive crime (Becker 1968; Ehrlich 1973). The key issue in understanding the influence of underground markets on acquisitive crime, then, concerns the conditions that shape the demand for stolen goods.

Research on illicit drug markets has considered their demand characteristics in some detail (Reuter 2010). Research on markets for stolen goods is more limited, especially with respect to how changes in the formal economy affect their expansion and contraction over time. Obtaining systematic time-series data on such markets is difficult, of course, because detailed records are rarely kept, but relevant insights can be drawn from observations of change in the retail sector of the formal economy. Generally speaking, when aggregate incomes fall or prices rise, consumers search for cheaper goods and services, a phenomenon economists refer to as "trading down." For example, as prices increase, midlevel retail outlets typically lose customers to those selling the same or similar goods at discount prices, such as Walmart and other "big-box" discount outlets, "dollar" stores, and the retail shops operated by Goodwill Industries and the Salvation Army.

But where do those who had been shopping at Dollar General or Goodwill trade down when the economy sours? Although the evidence trail leaves off at the bottom rungs of the formal retail market, a reasonable inference from the foregoing is that some enter the underground economy, including the market for stolen goods, in search of lower prices.

The cardinal quality of stolen merchandise is that it is cheap. If it were not, it would attract few consumers away from legal markets that sell the same products with purity and quality guarantees, return and replacement policies, peaceful procedures for resolving disputes, and no risk of arrest.

Inflation is not the only condition that influences the demand for stolen goods, but its effects are likely to be stronger and more direct than those of unemployment, economic growth, and income, especially when wages fail to keep pace with prices. In contrast with unemployment, the crime-relevant effects of inflation are widespread, instantaneous, and direct. The official unemployment rate, which excludes discouraged workers and others who have dropped out of the labor force, is a narrow and incomplete measure of joblessness.

But even broader measures such as labor-force participation necessarily apply only to persons who are out of work (and their families) and do not capture the effects of changing economic conditions on those who remain employed, who constitute the large majority of the working-age population even under the worst economic circumstances. In addition, the full effects of job loss typically develop over a period of months, as savings are drawn down and unemployment insurance benefits are exhausted (Cantor and Land 1985). By contrast, although its effects are greatest for the poor, inflation touches all consumers.

In a national-level US study, Rosenfeld and Levin (2016) found strong support for the effect of inflation on change over time in "acquisitive" crime, offenses committed for monetary gain (robbery and property offenses). The higher the inflation rate, the higher the acquisitive crime rate. As the inflation rate decreased, so did acquisitive crime. The inflation effects were more robust than the effects of economic growth and unemployment and they persisted over several years. Only two other variables rivaled the impact of inflation on acquisitive crime: consumer sentiment and the imprisonment rate. Other things equal, declining acquisitive crime rates were associated with increases in consumers' optimism about the state of the economy and their own economic fortunes, and they were related to growth in the prison population.

Recent research has also revealed significant effects of inflation on trends in acquisitive crime and homicide in a sample of US cities during the past several decades (Rosenfeld and Vogel 2023; Rosenfeld et al. 2019). The researchers found that the effect of inflation on homicide was partially mediated by acquisitive crime. In other words, inflation had a significant effect on acquisitive crime which, in turn, had a significant effect on homicide. The reasons why robbery and property crimes can influence the homicide rate were discussed in Section 2. But the effect of inflation on homicide was only partially mediated by acquisitive crime; a significant and sizable direct effect of inflation on homicide remained after taking account of its indirect effect through acquisitive crime. Rosenfeld and Vogel (2023) speculated that inflation also affected homicide through its impact on institutional legitimacy.

## 6.2 Crime, Inflation, and Institutional Legitimacy

The criminologist Gary LaFree maintained that rates of homicide and other crimes will increase when social institutions lose their legitimacy (LaFree 1998). Strong institutions discourage crime by guiding behavior into socially approved channels. When institutional supports for normative behavior and controls over disapproved behavior weaken, crime rates go up. Institutions rely for their effective performance on public confidence. If confidence wanes, behavior becomes unmoored from its institutional guideposts. LaFree (1998) observed that public confidence in political and economic institutions plummeted during the 1960s and 1970s amid racial tensions and disorder in US cities, widespread protests against the Vietnam War, and the Watergate crisis that brought down a president.[17] As a consequence, crime rates climbed.

Another major culprit was rampant inflation which, according to LaFree (1998), undermined public confidence in both the economy and government during the 1960s and 1970s. Surveys conducted during the 1990s in the United States and Germany found that respondents in both countries believed that inflation is both a consequence and a cause of political instability and that it damages national cohesion and prestige, in addition to reducing living standards (Shiller 1997). The research on crime, inflation, and institutional legitimacy makes an important contribution to the theory of crime trends discussed in the following section.

In summary, inflation affects crime trends in at least two ways: by increasing the demand for and supply of cheap stolen goods and by destabilizing social institutions. The small, but growing, literature on crime trends and inflation (see Rosenfeld and Levin, 2016, for a review) offers strong support for including inflation in future research on why crime rates change over time.

## 7 Crime Trends and the Institutional Order

Social institutions are the heart of a macrocriminology of crime trends. Institutions specify the values and norms, the "rules of the game," that channel social behavior. Institutions in this sense are distinct from the organizations that constitute them. Education is an institution; universities are organizations. Police departments and prisons are organizations; the criminal justice system is an institution. Several important implications flow from this conceptualization of institutions for the study of crime in general and crime trends in particular.

The form and frequency of criminal behavior will differ depending on features of the institutional order. As such, patterns and levels of crime are likely to vary across different historical periods, following the currents of social change. It follows that, in a fundamental sense, crime is normal (Durkheim 1966 [1895]). Every society thus has a normal rate of crime, that is, the crime rate generated by the prevailing institutional order. Moreover, notwithstanding historical variability in levels and forms of crime, the crime rate can never be driven to zero. Even as some types of crime fall over time, others rise. For example, violent crime rates have declined in most Western societies since the Middle Ages, but rates of property crime have increased over the same period (Eisner 2001; Shelley 1981).

---

[17] For example, Gallup surveys found that the percentage of respondents who had a "great deal" or "quite a lot" of confidence in Congress fell from 50% in 1973 to 32% in 1981 (https://news .gallup.com/poll/1597/confidence-institutions.aspx).

Finally, the social normality of crime implies that crime rates may fall too low for the effective operation of a society. As Durkheim (1966 [1895] maintained: "There is no occasion for self-congratulation when the crime rate drops below the average level, for we may be certain that this apparent progress is associated with some social disorder" (72). A recent example is the drop in robberies, burglaries, and larcenies at the height of the Covid-19 pandemic in the United States. With fewer people on the street, there are fewer suitable targets for street robbers. When people stay at home because they are unemployed, home burglaries decrease. When the shops are closed, there is limited opportunity for shoplifting (Rosenfeld and Lopez 2022). The pandemic was a "social disorder" that reduced crime rates below their normal levels.

## 7.1 Institutional Analysis of Crime Trends

An exciting development in criminological theory over the past few decades has been the renewed attention devoted to the role of social institutions, a development that has been termed the "new institutionalism" in criminology (Karstedt 2010). This new institutionalism has been manifested most prominently in recent research on criminal punishment (e.g., Garland 1990, 2001). Institutional analysis also has an important role to play in the study of crime trends.

Three dimensions of social institutions are particularly important when analyzing the implications of the institutional order for change over time in crime rates: institutional *structure*, institutional *regulation*, and institutional *performance* (see Messner et al. 2011). Institutional structure encompasses the content of the institutional rules and their internal consistency. An example is the emphasis on individual economic achievement under conditions of open, competitive mobility inherent in the value complex known as the "American Dream." A competitive, profit-oriented capitalist economy channels social action in accordance with this value complex (Messner and Rosenfeld 2013).

Institutional regulation refers to the basis of compliance with the rules. Not all action in conformity with institutional norms is "institutionalized" in the formal sense of the term. Individuals may align their behavior with the rules of the game based on strictly utilitarian calculations of self-interest or in response to coercive pressures by the more powerful. The distinctive feature of institutionalized social action is that it is governed by a sense of obligation; individuals act in accordance with the rules because they believe it is the right thing to do. When institutional regulation is strong, the rules of the game are granted considerable legitimacy.

The procedural justice literature in criminology provides a good example of institutional regulation (Tyler 1990; Tyler et al. 2015). When individuals perceive their treatment by the police to be fair, impartial, respectful, and just, they

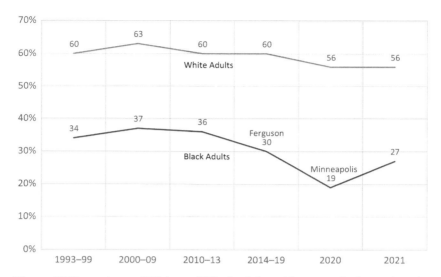

**Figure 10** Percentage of White and Black adults with a great deal or quite a lot of confidence in the police, 1993–2021.

**Source:** Gallup Poll

are more likely to willingly comply with the law. When people believe treatment is unjust, compliance is less likely or occurs under conditions of duress. Confidence in the police fell among Black Americans after two incidents of police violence that were widely perceived to be unjust: the killings of Michael Brown in Ferguson, Missouri, in 2014 and George Floyd in Minneapolis in 2020 (see Figure 10).[18] Confidence in the police among Black Americans rose in 2021, but not to the level that prevailed prior to the Ferguson killing. Meanwhile, confidence in the police among White Americans dropped only slightly after these incidents. Homicide rates increased in both the Black and White population in 2015 and 2020 (see Figure 5), but any causal connection between the decrease in confidence and the increase in homicide remains uncertain.[19]

It is also apparent from Figure 10 that confidence in the police among Black Americans has been much lower than in the White population for at least the past three decades and undoubtedly longer. Lack of confidence in the police is related to a pervasive and long-standing "legal cynicism" in highly

---

[18]  https://news.gallup.com/poll/352304/black-confidence-police-recovers-2020-low.aspx.

[19]  One study found little impact of the social unrest following a highly controversial instance of police behavior, the death of Freddie Gray while being transported by Baltimore police, on measures of trust in the police and procedural justice among Baltimore residents (White et al. 2018).

disadvantaged Black communities (Hagan et al. 2020; Kirk and Papachristos 2015; Sampson and Bartusch 1998). According to this research, legal cynicism and lack of confidence in the police are not an outgrowth of the "culture" of these communities, the values and beliefs that constitute their institutional structure in the terms of the current discussion. Rather, they reflect institutional deregulation, a loss of the fervor and force of the cultural rules such that compliance, if it occurs at all, is the product of strictly utilitarian considerations or has to be compelled by force.

Institutional performance concerns the extent to which commitment to and faithful enactment of institutional roles result in the expected institutional outcomes. Performance suffers when institutions fail to "deliver the goods." Generally speaking, institutional performance is most relevant for understanding short-run changes in crime rates, as when an increase in inflation or consumer pessimism results in an increase in crime (Rosenfeld and Levin 2016). But if disruptions in institutional performance persist over many years or decades, they can weaken institutional regulation by reducing confidence in existing institutional arrangements and, on occasion, fomenting a legitimacy crisis, as was the case during the 1960s and 1970s in the United States (LaFree 1998). Roth (2009) presents several examples in American history of crime increases associated with declining confidence in the federal government. Finally, severe institutional crises can lead to fundamental alterations in the institutional order and ignite crime increases during the transition to a new set of institutional arrangements, as occurred after the fall of the Soviet Union (Pridemore and Kim 2006).

Institutional structure, regulation, and performance are distal sources of change in crime rates. Further theoretical development will require specification of more proximate conditions. Baumer et al. (2018) offered a "blueprint" that outlines several more proximate sources of change in crime rates and that can be situated in the institutional framework outlined here. Their blueprint also would bring a theory of crime trends to the center of mainstream criminological theory.

Baumer et al. (2018) proposed that crime trends can be understood on the basis of three related concepts: social controls, individual criminal propensities and motivations, and criminal opportunities. Each concept is rooted in one or another mainstream criminological perspective. Social control theory holds that delinquent and criminal behavior results when individuals' attachment and commitment to, and involvement and belief in, conventional groups and institutions are weakened or absent (Hirschi 1969; Kornhauser 1978). Anomie and strain theories locate the motivations for crime in blocked goals and negative emotions (Agnew 2005; Merton 1938). Self-control theory stipulates that criminal propensities are a product of impulsivity, weak social attachments, and poor parenting (Gottfredson and Hirschi 1990). Rational choice and routine activity theories explain criminal activity in terms of rational cost-benefit calculations by motivated offenders in "criminogenic settings" where suitable victims are present and capable guardians are absent (Cohen and Felson 1979; Cornish and Clarke 1986).

Centering crime trends theory in mainstream criminological theories helps to reveal the institutional moorings of each of the three proximate sources of change in crime rates. Social control, both formal and informal, is a basic function of institutions and is the primary means by which behavior is channeled into normative pathways. Families exert normative controls through the socialization process. The free market economy exerts remunerative controls through the wage and profit system, although this type of control is prone to institutional deregulation by fostering compliance based on self-serving utilitarian grounds (Messner and Rosenfeld 2013). The criminal justice system exerts normative or coercive controls, depending on the legitimacy accorded to its procedures.

Anomie theories link the motivation to commit or refrain from crime both to the structure of social institutions and to institutional performance. Messner and Rosenfeld (2013) maintained that commitment to the values inherent in the American Dream promotes crime when institutional controls are weakened. Merton (1938) famously proposed that criminal adaptations can result when adherence to the dominant rules of the game does not lead to expected rewards. Cohen and Felson (1979) argued that the institutional changes that emptied homes by bringing women into the paid labor force altered the opportunity structure for crime and led to increases in residential burglaries.

Other changes in criminal opportunities, however, are less closely tied to the structure, regulation, or performance of social institutions. Modifications to the physical environment and consumer products, such as shielding shopkeepers behind heavy glass and installing electronic locking and ignition systems in motor vehicles, can reduce opportunities for crime in the absence of institutional change. That said, a broad-scale "safety consciousness" has taken off in the United States and elsewhere in recent decades, propelled in no small measure by the public health profession. Safety consciousness involves inspecting every aspect of the physical and social environment for potential hazards and eliminating them through environmental or product redesign – what criminologists term "target hardening." An example is the secure storage of firearms so that children cannot gain access to them (Coyne-Beasley et al. 2002). To the extent that the reduction of criminal opportunities is part of this broader shift in institutional structure, it too belongs in a theory of crime trends and the institutional order.

The "new institutionalism" in criminology serves as a sturdy basis for the development of a macrolevel theory of crime trends. Crime rates move up and down over time as a consequence of changes in the institutional order of societies – most of the time. Sometimes, however, crime rates undergo sharp and abrupt shifts for reasons that cannot be anticipated by even the most comprehensive theory or the most reliable research methods. These changes are produced by "exogenous shocks" to the social order.

## 8 Bumps along the Way: Crime Trends and Exogenous Shocks

Most research on crime trends consists of "normal science" studies of relatively slow change in crime over time in relation to comparably gradual and more or less expected changes in criminal opportunities, incentives, and penalties.[20] New empirical indicators are discovered or devised that better fit underlying concepts and propositions, new results complement or supplant older ones. But crime rates sometimes behave in ways that defy expectations from the normal science of crime trends. These unexpected and abrupt changes in crime rates require new ways of thinking about temporal shifts in crime. Simply incorporating new empirical indictors into the same old explanatory models is not sufficient; the models themselves have to be replaced. That is the challenge posed by exogenous shocks to theory and research on crime trends. An example is the recent rise in homicide rates in the United States.

As shown in Figure 1, the US homicide rate rose by 30% in 2020, the largest percentage increase in a single year on record (Rosenfeld and Lopez 2022). But this was not the only notable homicide rise in recent years. The homicide rate increased by 11.4% between 2014 and 2015, the largest yearly percentage increase since 1968 (Rosenfeld et al. 2017). The explanations, constructs, and tools of the normal science of crime trends were not prepared for these recent homicide spikes. They were too large, abrupt, and unexpected to be explained by the typically slow-moving variables in standard econometric models of crime rates. Whatever events or conditions had caused the homicide rise had to themselves have changed very rapidly. They had to be shocks to the long-run change in homicide rates associated with changing demographic, economic, and institutional conditions, although they may have interacted with those conditions in their effects.

No widely accepted, evidence-based explanation exists for these sudden shifts in the homicide rate. Nonetheless, two likely candidates for the exogenous shocks are (1) the Covid-19 outbreak in 2020 and (2) an increase in police–community tensions and social unrest in the aftermath of widely publicized and

---

[20] This section draws from Rosenfeld (2018).

controversial incidents of police use of deadly force against minorities. The lockdowns and quarantines instituted in the first months of the pandemic altered day-to-day living patterns in ways that, on balance, reduced opportunities for street crime, including homicide (Lopez and Rosenfeld 2021). But homicide rates rose precipitously in 2020, pushed up by conditions that evidently overrode the crime-reducing effects of the alterations in population mobility related to the pandemic. One such condition may have been an increase in violent motivations stimulated by the psychological stress and social dislocations of the pandemic itself. Another popular explanation for both of the recent homicide spikes points to frustrations, demoralization, and anger that caused police to back away from proactive engagement in their duties – a deinstitutionalization of policing – that was labeled the "Ferguson effect" during the homicide rise in 2015 (Mac Donald 2016; Rosenfeld et al. 2017) and the "Minneapolis Effect" in 2020 (Cassell 2020).

There is no doubt that fewer police officers were fully engaged in their jobs at the height of the pandemic. But that was largely because of the pandemic itself. Many officers were away from work because they were sick themselves or had been exposed to someone with the virus. Those who remained on the job were subject to agency protocols or used their own discretion to maintain safe distance from citizens on the street. Surveys conducted in the early days of the pandemic found that law enforcement agencies across the country substantially reduced in-person responses to calls for service and also cut back on arrests, proactive policing, and community policing (Lum et al. 2022). The best evidence suggests that reduced policing was not a "Minneapolis Effect" so much as a Covid effect.

An alternative version of the policing explanation for the homicide rise switches the focus from police behavior to community attitudes and beliefs. As discussed earlier, people who trust the police endow their legal authority with legitimacy. When the police lack legitimacy, people tend to avoid them, are less likely to contact them to settle interpersonal disputes, and are more likely to seek private vengeance (Tyler et al. 2015). Alienation from the means of formal social control gives rise to pervasive legal cynicism, the emergence of violence-condoning "honor cultures," and peremptory and retaliatory violence, especially in economically disadvantaged communities lacking access to alternative forms of protection and conflict resolution.

This explanation directs attention to the long history of fraught relationships between the police and communities of color in the United States. A reservoir of discontent with the police stretches back to the slave patrols and police enforcement of Jim Crow segregation laws. But how can it explain the sudden rise in homicide in 2015 and then again in 2020? The spark that set the reservoir aflame, in this rendering of the policing narrative, was the upsurge in controversial incidents of police brutality and social unrest in Ferguson, Baltimore, Chicago, Minneapolis, and elsewhere across the country.

Exogenous shocks to crime trends are not new. An example is the crack epidemic that sparked a sharp rise in youth violence in the late 1980s, reversing the previous trajectory of crime rates (Blumstein 1995; Cook and Laub 1998). Eventually, however, exogenous shocks tend to succumb to the constraints of normal science. That does not necessarily end debates about their causes, but the debates are fought on firmer scientific ground. The same is beginning to occur in the case of the more recent homicide spikes (see, e.g., Rogers et al. 2023). What is certain, however, is that exogenous shocks will continue to upset expectations about temporal changes in crime rates derived from the theories, methods, and models of normal science. They also pose a challenge to our ability to predict future crime rates, the topic of the following section.

## 9 Forecasting Crime Rates

*It is like holding a small candle in a hurricane to see if there are any paths ahead and how to go forth. But if one cannot light and hold even a small candle then there is only darkness before us.*

Daniel Bell[21]

When criminologists are asked what will happen to crime rates in the near future, we are often left speechless.[22] It is not a senseless question. Economists are asked the same question about economic conditions all the time, and they usually have an answer based on economic forecasting models. Crime forecasts have never been widespread in criminology, but they have all but disappeared in recent years.[23] The current unpopularity of crime forecasting is likely attributable to the wildly inaccurate forecasts by ostensible experts of an impending crime boom just as crime rates were beginning their historic drop in the early 1990s. James Alan Fox, then dean of the Northeastern University College of Criminal Justice, wrote: "The worst is yet to come. I believe we are on the verge of a crime wave that will last into the next century" (quoted in Schuster 1995). Princeton University political scientist and criminologist John DiIullio (1995) coined the term "superpredator" to describe the morally impoverished youth

---

[21] Quoted in Waters (1996: 164).

[22] This section draws from Rosenfeld and Berg (2023).

[23] Recent interest in predictive policing is something of an exception, but it is limited to short-run (time of day, days, weeks) forecasts in crime hot spots and other small urban spaces. Predictive policing algorithms have been criticized for lack of methodological transparency, racial bias, and ineffectiveness in reducing crime (Lau 2020). Gorr et al. (2003) used more traditional forecasting methods to forecast crime rates in Pittsburgh police districts one month ahead.

who would fuel the looming crime boom (see, also, Haberman 2014). This was not criminology's finest hour.

The problem with the inaccurate crime forecasts of the 1990s was not that they were inaccurate. The problem was that they were not based on a verifiable model of crime trends, or any model at all, other than single-factor projections of the size of the adolescent population. The mistakes of thirty years ago need not be repeated and should not deter renewed efforts at crime forecasting. If the study of crime trends is to have policy relevance, it will come mainly from forecasting. Policymakers have an interest in past crime rates mainly in so far as they portend future changes. The planning horizon for criminal justice policy rarely extends beyond a few years, and forecasting models should be calibrated accordingly.

But just because policymakers are interested in the near future of crime rates does not necessarily mean that there are clear, actionable steps from crime forecasts to policy, and certainly not the tight coupling with policy that exists for forecasts of the weather, economic conditions, and disease.[24] A warning system is activated and remedial actions are undertaken when forecasts indicate a serious storm, economic downturn, or an infectious disease is on the way. No such policy infrastructure and consequent demand for actionable intelligence exist with respect to crime forecasting.

But is that a reason to forgo crime forecasting for policy purposes or to build the infrastructure? This is not a technical question but a question of political will and responsiveness. I think the public would like to be forewarned about increases in crime rates and to assume that policymakers are prepared to respond effectively to anticipated problems (e.g., overcrowded jails, prisons, and court calendars, police shortages, underresourced crime prevention programs). One thing is clear: the primary impediment to bringing crime forecasting to bear on crime policy is *not* the accuracy of the forecasts. Forecasts of all kinds are often inaccurate. The expected uptick in unemployment doesn't happen, the storm weakens before landfall, the illness is milder than anticipated. Economic, environmental, and health policymakers do not abandon forecasts and early warning systems in these areas because they are inaccurate; they work to improve them. The same should be true for crime.

Forecasting models will always contain error of two general types. They may be inaccurate (the crime rate falls outside the forecast range) or imprecise (the crime rate is within the forecast range, but the range is so broad it has little practical utility). The errors then become the basis for revising the models. Despite the inevitable errors, crime forecasts derived from explicable statistical models should

---

[24] I thank Eric Baumer for this making important point in a personal communication.

usually outperform guesswork. Even if they do not, they enable the investigator to determine the sources of the forecasting error and re-specify the models.

Finally, crime forecasting is the most exacting way to test hypotheses about changes in crime rates. To avoid over fitting the data used to develop them, theories should always be evaluated with "out-of-sample" observations. The typical way of testing a theoretical model of the change over time in crime rates is to determine how it fits the data used to generate the model – in other words, data on *past* crime rates. This is a necessary, but not sufficient, method of theory testing. A more demanding test is to determine how well the model predicts *future* crime rates. This test does not require waiting until the future arrives. It simply requires reserving some data from the sample used to generate the model to see how well it predicts these out-of-sample observations. I perform such a validation exercise in forecasts of New York City violent and property crime rates in this section.

## 9.1 Background

A literature search produced just eight macrolevel studies that include forecasts of crime rates in the United States and none that were published in the last fifteen years.[25] The oldest study was published almost fifty years ago (Fox 1978), and the most recent studies appeared in 2008 (Baumer 2008; Pepper 2008). The strong focus of most of the studies is on how projected changes in the age composition of the population are expected to influence future crime rates, although some investigations incorporate additional factors, such as unemployment, imprisonment, and policing (Cohen and Land 1987; Cohen et al. 1980; Fox 1978). A study by Land and McCall (2001) is particularly noteworthy because it devotes explicit and sustained attention to the assumptions and challenges of forecasting crime rates.

Land and McCall (2001) pointed out that all crime forecasts are prone to uncertainty owing to the simple fact that the future is unknowable until it arrives. Crime forecasters, therefore, should avoid "point forecasts" that predict a single future crime rate. Instead, researchers should employ a range of forecasts or "forecast cones" bounded by upper and lower limits that can be estimated in different ways and usually involve expert judgment regarding the future conditions likely to affect crime rates. They also cautioned against "continuity bias" in crime forecasts that are "heavily influenced by recent trends in crime rates just prior to the period for which the forecasts are made" (344). They recommended that forecast periods should be as short as possible, no more than a few years ahead, to reduce forecasting error and in recognition of the abbreviated budget and planning horizons of most policymakers, especially at

---

[25] Baumer (2008); Cohen and Land (1987); Cohen et al. (1980); Fox (1978); Fox and Piquero (2003); Land and McCall (2001); Pepper (2008); Steffensmeier and Harer (1987).

the local level. Their final recommendation is to update forecasts as often as possible as new data become available (345).

Land and McCall (2001) engaged in a forecasting exercise based on these suggestions. They forecasted the number of 14- to 17-year-old Black male homicide offenders and the number of same-age White male homicide offenders in the United States for each year from 1998 to 2007. The forecasts were based on the homicide offending rates of the two groups of adolescents from 1980 to 1987 and Census Bureau projections of the size of each group through the forecast period. They set the lower bound of forecasting cones for each group at 25% of their lowest homicide offending rate between 1980 and 1987 and the upper bound at 125% of their highest 1980–1987 homicide offending rate. The midrange forecast assumed their average 1980–1987 offending rate would remain constant throughout the forecast period.

The resulting forecasts cover a very wide range of estimated outcomes. For example, by 2002, midway through the forecast period, the estimated number of White homicide offenders ranged from fewer than 100 at the lower limit of the forecast cone to about 3,800 at the upper limit. The midlevel estimate was about 500 (341, Figure B). Land and McCall (2001) did not offer strong reasons why the midlevel forecast should be preferred over the upper and lower limits of the forecast cone; the key point of the exercise is to avoid single-point forecasting. Their forecast cones for adolescent male homicide offenders are likely to be very accurate but so imprecise they would have little practical utility. The solution is not to favor point forecasts over a range of estimates, but to create forecast cones with boundaries that are narrow enough for policy purposes but wide enough to produce accurate forecasts. Useful and reliable forecasting, in other words, always involves a tradeoff between precision and accuracy.

This section presents a forecasting exercise using time series data on violent and property crime rates in New York City. The main point of the exercise is not to correctly predict New York crime rates, although the forecasts are evaluated for their accuracy and precision. Rather, the primary purpose of the exercise is to explore the feasibility of and challenges to crime forecasting. The section concludes that, while the challenges are considerable, the benefits of crime forecasting, for both researchers and policymakers, outweigh them. It is time for a revival of crime forecasting in criminology.

## 9.2 Data and Methods

The forecasting exercise is carried out with Land's and McCall's (2001) thoughtful discussion of the dos and don'ts of crime forecasting in mind. As they point out, because criminal justice policymaking is largely a local matter in the United States, crime forecasting is better done at the local than the national level. This exercise, therefore, is based on data for the city of New York. The outcomes are New York's violent crime rate (murder, rape, robbery, and aggravated assault) and property crime rate (burglary, larceny, and motor vehicle theft). The sample data span the period 1980 to 2016.

Two out-of-sample forecast periods are examined. The first is the period between 2017 and 2021. This five-year out-of-sample period, during which New York's violent and property crime rates are known, is used to validate the forecasts derived from a model based on the 1980–2016 data. The violent and property crime rates for 2022 to 2024 are then forecasted. The crime rates for this period were unknown when these analyses were carried out. The forecasting exercise is summarized in the text, and technical details can be found in Appendix II.

### 9.2.1 Forecast Methods

A first step in forecasting the values of a time series is to evaluate the series for "stationarity." A stationary series is one in which the mean and variance of the series are constant or nearly so over time. Forecasts of a stationary time series are more reliable than those of a nonstationary series. Statistical tests confirmed that the violent and property crime rate time series are nonstationary.

A common approach to transforming a nonstationary time series to a stationary series is to first difference the series. First differencing transforms a series measured in levels (in this case, crime rates) to one in which each data point is the difference between the variable's current value and previous value (i.e., $Y_t - Y_{t-1}$). Second and higher-order differencing can be applied if first differencing does not produce stationarity. First differencing was sufficient to produce stationarity in the violent and property crime series.

Autoregressive integrated moving average (ARIMA) models were used to forecast the first-differenced violent and property crime rates. ARIMA models are commonly used in forecasting because they offer a thorough assessment of the properties of a time series (Hyndman and Athanasopoulos 2018). The multivariate ARIMA models were specified in line with the analysis of US crime data by Rosenfeld and Levin (2016). A parsimonious model was created that contains the two variables with the most robust effects on crime rates in the Rosenfeld and Levin study: the inflation rate and the imprisonment rate. The effects of inflation should worsen to the degree that incomes do not keep pace with price increases, and so the inflation rate is adjusted for median household income (inflation/median income). The imprisonment rate is lagged one year behind the crime rate. Lagging the imprisonment rate helps to mitigate but does

*Criminology*

**Table 1** Descriptive statistics (N=37).

| Variable | Mean St. | Dev. | Min | Max |
|---|---|---|---|---|
| Violent Crime Rate | 1312.24 | 681.74 | 568.20 | 2383.60 |
| Property Crime Rate | 4145.98 | 2444.52 | 1467.40 | 8007.30 |
| Inflation Rate | 3.52 | 2.24 | .10 | 11.40 |
| Md Household Income (000) | 36.82 | 12.35 | 13.85 | 58.86 |
| Income-Adjusted Inflation | .14 | .16 | .00 | .82 |
| Prison Rate | 698.54 | 169.19 | 308.50 | 917.70 |

**Notes:** Period=1980–2016
Variable definitions:
Violent Crime Rate=Violent crimes per 100,000 population
Property Crime Rate=Property crimes per 100,000 population
Inflation Rate=Percentage change in Consumer Price Index
Md Household Income (000)=Median household income in thousands of dollars
Income-Adjusted Inflation=Inflation Rate/Md Household Income (000)
Prison Rate=State prisoners per 100,000 population
Data sources described in the text.

not fully eliminate the estimation error associated with the endogeneity of imprisonment, as discussed in Section 3.

The inflation rate is for the New York City metropolitan area, and the imprisonment rate is for the state of New York.[26] The New York inflation rates for 2023 and 2024 and income and imprisonment values for 2022 to 2024 were unknown. The inflation rates were assumed to be equal to national inflation forecasts from the Congressional Budget Office (www.cbo.gov/data/budget-economic-data#4). Income and imprisonment values were estimated from ARIMA forecast models discussed in Appendix II.

## 9.3 Results

Descriptive statistics for the variables (in original metric) used in this analysis are shown in Table 1. The violent and property crime rates exhibit substantial variation over the 1980–2016 observation period. Both trended downward over time. The highest violent crime rate during the period, 2383.6 violent crimes per 100,000 population in 1990, was more than four times greater than the lowest rate, 568.2 per 100,000 in 2009. The highest property crime rate, 8007.3 per 100,000 in 1981, was over five times greater than the lowest rate, 1467.4 per

---

[26] The inflation data are from the Bureau of Labor Statistics (www.bls.gov/regions/new-york-new-jersey/news-release/consumerpriceindex_newyorkarea.htm). The crime and imprisonment data are from the FBI's Uniform Crime Reports and the New York State Division of Criminal Justice Services (www.criminaljustice.ny.gov).

100,000 in 2016. The explanatory variables exhibit comparable or even greater variation during the observation period.

New York's violent and property crime rates between 1980 and 2016 are displayed in Figure 11. To eliminate scale differences and reveal the relationship between the trends in the two crime types, they are scaled on separate axes, with violent crime on the left-hand axis and property crime on the right-hand axis of the figure. Both violent and property crime rates fell during the early 1980s and rose during the next few years, before falling continuously well into the current century during what has been termed the "Great American Crime Decline" (Zimring 2007). What is also striking about the violent and property crime time trends is how closely they correspond (the Pearson's correlation (r) between the two series is .98). This high degree of convergence suggests that the same sources of change over time in New York's violent crime rate also underlie the change in the property crime rate.

Figure 11 provides clear visual confirmation that New York's violent and property crime rates between 1980 and 2016 are nonstationary; the mean rates decrease over time. The forecast models were therefore fit to the first-differenced violent and property crime rates between 1980 and 2016. The years 2017 to 2021 were "held back" from the models so they could be used to validate the forecasts from the 1980–2015 baseline period. The closer the forecasted crime rates are to

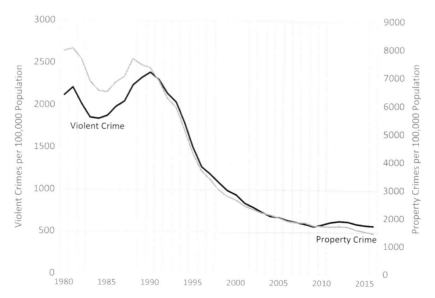

**Figure 11** New York violent and property crime rates, 1980–2016.

**Source:** New York State Division of Criminal Justice Services; Uniform Crime Reports

the observed rates during the validation period, the greater our confidence in the forecasts for 2022 to 2024 when the crime rates are unknown.

The forecasting results are presented in Figures 12 and 13 (and Table A-1 in Appendix II). The figures display the observed and forecasted values of the crime series from 2000 to 2024. The solid line denotes the observed values from 2000 to 2021. The dashed line denotes the forecasts for 2000 to 2016, the dotted line indicates the forecasts for 2017 to 2021, the validation period, and the gray-shaded dotted line represents the forecasts for 2022 to 2024. In 2017, the first year of the forecast validation period, the New York's observed violent crime rate dropped by 37 violent crimes per 100,000 population, while the forecasted rate shows little change. The changes in the observed and forecasted violent crime rates are fairly close during the next few years until 2021, when the observed rate increased by more than 80 violent crimes per 100,000, and the forecasted rate drops by about 25 violent crimes per 100,000. The forecasts indicate that New York's violent crime rate should rise in 2022 and 2023. The rate in 2024 should exhibit little change over the previous year.

As shown in Figure 13, New York's observed and forecasted first-differenced property crime rates are very similar between 2017 and 2021. In 2017, they diverge by 66 property crimes per 100,000, by 34 in 2018 and 2019, and by just 19 in 2020. As with violent crime, the difference between the changes in the

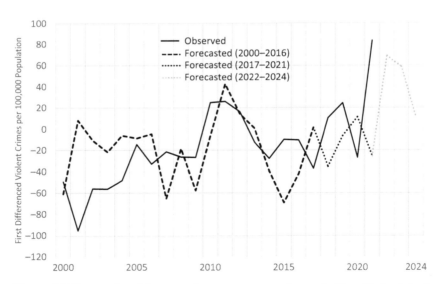

**Figure 12** Observed and forecasted year-over-year change in New York violent crime rate, 2000–2024.

**Source** for observed data: New York State Division of Criminal Justice Services; Uniform Crime Reports

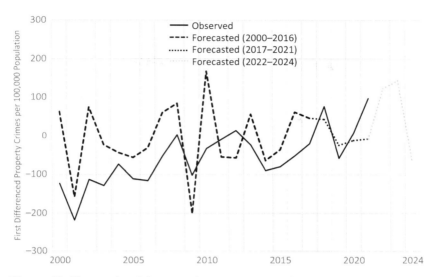

**Figure 13** Observed and forecasted year-over-year change New York property crime rate, 2000–2024.

**Source** for observed data: New York State Division of Criminal Justice Services; Uniform Crime Reports

observed and forecasted property crime rates is larger in 2021, when the observed rate grew by nearly 100 property crimes per 100,000, and the forecasted rate falls slightly. The forecasts suggest that New York's property crime rate should rise in 2022 and 2023 before falling in 2024.

Contrary to Land's and McCall's (2001) advice, this exercise yields point forecasts of New York's crime rates and not the kind of forecast cones they prefer. Nonetheless, it is important to create boundaries around the point forecasts to evaluate their utility for both policymaking and theory testing. This means that the policymaker or researcher will have to decide how much forecast error is tolerable, which is a substantive and not a statistical decision. We will assume for current purposes that forecasted crime rates that diverge from the observed rates by no more than 10% are sufficiently accurate and precise for both policy and theory evaluation. Forecasts that fall outside of these limits would be uninformative, although they do suggest that the forecast model probably needs to be revised.

The forecast errors for violent crime fall outside the 10% limits in 2021 and are inside the limits for the other years of the validation period (see Table A-1 in Appendix II). These results suggest that the forecast model for violent crime should be revisited to determine the source of the forecast error in 2021. One likely candidate is the exogenous shock to crime rates from the Covid-19 pandemic, which no forecast model could have predicted. In the meantime, a conservative approach would be to rely on the five-year mean forecasts instead of the yearly estimates for forecasting purposes. This would reduce the average forecasting errors during the validation period, but it would not capture the forecasted rise in violent crime rates from 2022 to 2024 estimated from the ARIMA model. A fair conclusion is that the forecasting results for violent crime are acceptably precise on average and that the large error during 2021 was unavoidable.

The story for property crime is somewhat different. The forecasted property crime rates during the validation period are well within the 10% tolerance limits. These limits were arbitrarily drawn, but even if the 10% divergence threshold were cut in half, the forecasted property crime rates would have been accurate and precise enough for both policy and research purposes between 2017 and 2020 and nearly so in 2021.

The forecasting results for New York's violent and property crime rates inspire guarded optimism about the prospects for forecasting in criminology. The forecasted property crime rates are very close to the observed rates during the validation period and provide a reliable basis for forecasting property crime rates three years ahead. The same is generally true for the violent crime results. The forecast error for violent crime in 2021, however, is outside the 10% tolerance limits placed around the estimates. More permissive limits could have been chosen, of course, but the optimal standard – how much error is acceptable – is not a statistical question but a matter of judgment and the preferred tradeoff between forecast accuracy and precision. The forecast error is also an important reminder of the challenge of unanticipated shocks to forecasting crime rates, or anything else.

## 9.4 Conclusion

Forecasting future crime rates, when done carefully on the basis of a credible forecasting model, is a natural and needed extension of the study of crime trends. Forecasting provides data to test theory that were not in the sample of observations used to develop the theory. Forecasting answers the perennial plea of policymakers, the press, and the public: You've told me what happened yesterday; now tell me what will happen tomorrow. The answers will not always be accurate or precise, but they will come from an explicable set of methods and decisions that assume that the probable future of crime rates is related to their past behavior and to expected changes in the conditions known to influence it.

Modesty is the best policy when forecasting crime rates. Forecasts will almost always be off the mark in the presence of exogenous shocks that sever the future from the past and that no forecasting model could have predicted. A recent example is the Covid-19 pandemic, which affected crime rates in complex ways (Lopez and Rosenfeld 2021). Forecasts will also be incorrect when the conditions known to influence the crime rate change in unexpected ways, such as the abrupt increase in inflation beginning in 2021 (Banerjee et al. 2023). That is why forecasts should always be tested against out-of-sample conditions that are known, the approach taken here, before taking on the unknowable future. A useful way of presenting the forecasts is in the form of conditional probabilities: If these conditions hold, then the crime rate will be X. When uncertainty exists regarding the future state of crime-generating conditions, as it usually does, a range of probabilities can be estimated. For example, all else equal, if the inflation rate is 3%, then the crime rate will be Y. If the inflation rate increases to 5% or 7%, the crime rate will be Z. These conditional probabilities offer another way to construct forecast cones around the point forecasts.

The forecasting exercise conducted here is intended to revive interest in crime forecasting in criminology. I have tried to be explicit about the reasoning behind each of the steps taken to (1) ready the data for reliable forecasting, (2) specify an explanatory model to be used in multivariate forecasting, (3) choose a forecasting model, and (4) interpret the results. Each of these decisions is open to criticism and alternative approaches. While I believe the data, methods, and models used here are useful for reviving discussion and analysis of crime forecasting, they can be augmented in several ways, such as by increasing sample size and incorporating additional covariates to reduce sampling error.[27] In addition, other types of forecasting models (e.g., exponential smoothing models, which give greater weight to more recent observations) should be applied to the study of crime trends and their performance should be assessed against the ARIMA methods used here.

Crime forecasting has fallen on hard times in criminology, but past mistakes should not prevent renewed attention to this important endeavor. There is much work to do, both technical and political. This study has barely scratched the surface of the rich forecasting literature in other fields.[28] Preparing the policy environment to make optimal use of crime forecasting will take years. Meanwhile, there are grounds for optimism. Enough is now known about the behavior of crime rates to support reliable short-run forecasts of the future. And

---

[27] Measures of age composition and unemployment were included in initial regression models, but neither was statistically significant or improved model fit.

[28] Several forecasting textbooks are available (e.g., Box et al. 2016; Brockwell and Davis 2016; Hyndman and Athanasopoulos 2018). The *Journal of Forecasting* provides examples of more advanced applications.

testing our theories against future crime rates is the best way to improve our explanations of the past.

## 10 The Future of Crime Trends Theory and Research

The future of theory and research on crime trends depends in large part on attracting more research scholars to this line of criminological inquiry, which will require advances in theory, data, research methods, and policy relevance. Before turning to these issues, this section summarizes the major trends in US crime rates during the past several decades and many of the factors underlying the trends that have been covered in this Element.

## 10.1 Summary of Crime Trends and Explanations

### 10.1.1 Violent and Property Crime Rates Have Moved Up and Down Together over Time

After falling or remaining flat since the end of the Second World War, both violent and property crime rates in the United States began a decades-long increase in the mid-1960s. The rates peaked around 1980 and then again in the early 1990s. Street crime rates then fell more or less continuously until 2015, when homicide rates reversed course and rose while property crime rates continued to decline. Another sharp increase in homicide occurred in 2020 at the height of the Covid-19 pandemic but, again, property crime continued to fall.

### 10.1.2 Homicide Trends Are Related to Trends in Property Crime, Firearm Availability, and Imprisonment

Property crime is a risk factor for homicide. Small changes in property crime rates can generate large changes in homicide rates. Firearm availability is another risk factor for homicide, but increases in homicide also drive up firearm acquisition. Decreases in crime are related to increases in imprisonment, but the effects are small and weaken at higher levels of imprisonment.

### 10.1.3 Group-Specific Homicide Trends Follow the General Trend in Homicide

Group-specific trends correspond with the general trend in homicide, suggesting that, despite sizable differences in the level of homicide by race, ethnicity, and gender, the common time trends in the group-specific homicide rates are related to similar underlying demographic and socioeconomic conditions.

Not all group-specific homicide trends are similar, however. During the crack cocaine epidemic of the late 1980s and early 1990s, homicide rates in the adolescent and young adult population rose while the rates among older adults were flat or fell. While intimate-partner homicide rates have decreased over time, the declines have been greater among males than females. The drop in intimate-partner homicide among males is related to rising divorce rates and increases in domestic violence services and resources.

### 10.1.4 Crime Trends Are the Product of Age, Period, and Cohort Effects

One reason crime rates rose in the 1960s and 1970s is that the baby boom birth cohorts were entering adolescence and young adulthood, the developmental period when crime rates peak. When the baby boomers aged out of their crime-prone years in the early 1980s, crime rates fell. Despite a continuing drop in the size of the adolescent and young-adult population, however, crime rates increased again in the late 1980s amid the crack cocaine epidemic. As the epidemic waned in the early 1990s, and despite prominent, but erroneous, predictions to the contrary, crime rates again reversed course and returned to levels not seen since the 1960s. The lesson is that the age composition of the population (the age effect) is only one of several factors underlying changes in crime rates over time. Others include the social, economic, and policy environment in which age cohorts are born (cohort effect) and the environment in which they mature into adulthood (period effect).

### 10.1.5 Some Economic Conditions Have Stronger Effects on Crime Trends than Others

One robust period effect on crime trends is the state of the economy. The effect differs, however, depending on the economic indicator under investigation. The long-standing indicator of choice, the unemployment rate, has been supplanted in more recent research by measures such as consumer sentiment and inflation that are more closely and consistently related to crime trends. The inflation rate, along with the imprisonment rate, also has proven helpful in forecasting violent and property crime rates in the city of New York.

### 10.1.6 Forecasting Belongs in the Future of Crime Trends Research and Crime Control Policy

Forecasting is the best way to assess explanations of crime trends and to inform policy development and evaluation. But, among other challenges, crime forecasts can be upended by exogenous shocks that produce abrupt and unexpected changes in crime rates. In addition, the systematic policy application of crime forecasts has yet to be developed. Nonetheless, a vibrant future for crime trends research will in no small measure require greater attention to forecasting. The most pressing issue the study of crime trends faces, however, is theory development.

## 10.2 Theory

There is no comprehensive macrolevel theory of change in crime rates. Mainstream criminological theories such as the anomie-strain, control, cultural, and routine activity perspectives are certainly pertinent, but mainly as second-order suppliers of ideas and empirical findings. They do not constitute the core of a theory of change, either separately or in combination. New theoretical ground will have to be broken.

Baumer et al. (2018) offer valuable ideas for consolidating existing criminological theories in a conceptual framework that would facilitate the development of a theory of crime trends and, in the process, move the study of crime trends closer to mainstream criminology. As indicated earlier, in my view this framework should be informed by the central propositions of the new institutionalism in criminology:

*Crime is a social fact to be explained by other social facts.*
*Crime is a normal feature of the institutional order.*
*The form and frequency of crime will change with the regular rhythms of institutional performance, the sway of institutional regulation, and transformations in institutional structure.*

Institutional-anomie theory (Messner and Rosenfeld 2013) comes close to the kind of institutional approach that is needed, but it was developed primarily to explain differences across societies in crime rates and not trends in crime within societies.

## 10.3 Data

Theory development and testing will also require improvements to existing data and methods. The FBI's Uniform Crime Reports constitute the main data source in contemporary crime trends research. Other key sources are the Bureau of Justice Statistics' National Crime Victimization Survey and homicide data from the FBI's Supplementary Homicide Reports and the National Vital Statistics System. A significant gap in each of these systems is coverage of crime changes in real time. The UCR and NIBRS data are disseminated nine to ten months after the collection year, and the victimization and vital statistics data are even less timely. For some studies and when crime rates are changing relatively slowly, a lack of timeliness in the release of crime data is not a problem. But when crime levels appear to be changing very rapidly, such as during the recent homicide spikes in the United States, up-to-date data are clearly needed to dispel misconceptions (e.g., homicide rates are higher than ever) and anchor public debate in evidence rather than anecdote or groundless innuendo. There is no technical reason why the FBI crime data cannot be disseminated a month or two after collection, as was done in the quarterly crime reports issued during the 1930s and again beginning in 2020 amid concerns of a major crime rise. Private entities such as the Council on Criminal Justice (Rosenfeld and Lopez 2022) and AH Datalytics (www.ahdatalytics.com/about-us/) should not have to fill the data void left by the nation's major governmental sources of crime data.

Baumer et al. (2018) offer several useful recommendations for strengthening the nation's crime data infrastructure, in addition to speeding up the dissemination of the data. They propose that quarterly or semiannual surveys compile data on crime, the criminal justice system, and demographic and socioeconomic conditions from representative samples jurisdictions across the country. The data should be sufficiently granular to track crime trends across areas within cities and should be supplemented by qualitative studies of communities that differ in crime trends and "criminogenic events" such as drug markets and plant closings. Moreover, Lauritsen (2023) recommends establishing a new crime data infrastructure that includes offenses beyond those currently reported to and recorded by local law enforcement agencies. These are tall orders and the multifaceted system would take years and substantial funding to implement. And if recent history is any indication, as discussed in Section 2, the road to a new system for compiling crime data could be quite bumpy.

## 10.4 Methods

Methodological advances are needed to better capture the nature of change in crime rates. New methods and ways of thinking about crime changes have emerged in microspatial research that can be adopted in macrolevel studies (see Hipp and Luo 2022). The microspatial study of crime has important, if underexplored, implications for crime trends theory and research. Crime is heavily concentrated in a small number of urban and, according to some studies, suburban spaces (Gill et al. 2017; Weisburd et al. 2012). Weisburd (2015) has argued that crime concentration is so pronounced, pervasive, and consistent across jurisdictions and over time it qualifies as a criminological "law." Strong research support exists for the microspatial concentration of crime (Braga et al. 2017). Where disagreement exists, it mainly involves questions about the best ways to measure crime concentration, the most appropriate microspatial unit of analysis, and the stability of crime concentration over time.

The macrolevel study of crime trends has much to learn from the micro-spatial study of crime concentration. The most important lesson is to decompose the units of analysis. National-level crime trends consist of the trends in subnational units such as cities and states, and the crime rates of different places do not necessarily travel at the same speed. Some places may have a disproportionate influence on the overall trends, and a critically important research task is to identify the sources of spatial variability in the movement of crime rates over time.

Group-based trajectory methods, originally developed to analyze individual developmental differences in antisocial behavior, have been applied in micro-spatial crime research and hold great promise for advancing the macrolevel study of crime trends (Nagin 2005; Weisburd et al. 2004). These methods identify distinct clusters of persons or places on the basis of the trajectory over time of some outcome (e.g., antisocial behavior, crime rate). One question to which these methods can be productively applied is whether city crime rates follow a common national trend. McDowall and Lofin (2009) found this to be true in the United States. Baumer and Wolfe (2014) essentially confirmed this result, but their study uncovered somewhat greater heterogeneity in the movement of city crime rates over time and across different crime types. Group-based trajectory methods can be used to identify coherent clusters of cities that differ in their trends and in the demographic, socioeconomic, and policy attributes that underlie their distinct trajectories.

Finally, the trajectory methods can also enrich crime forecasting by identifying subtypes of places for which forecasts are more or less accurate and precise. It bears repeating that forecasting crime rates is a logical and, in my view, necessary next step in the macrolevel study of crime trends. Crime forecasting and trajectory analysis, of course, will always have to contend with exogenous shocks that can upset predictions from the most reliable models. In this respect, the criminologist is in a situation similar to British Prime Minister Harold Macmillan's who, when asked by a journalist what was the greatest challenge for a statesman, is reputed to have replied: "Events, dear boy, events."[29] With credible forecasting methods and models in place, however, and mindful of the uncertainties thrown up by unforeseen events, the study of crime trends can secure its future.

---

[29] www.oxfordreference.com/display/10.1093/acref/9780199916108.001.0001/acref-9780199916108-e-2597;jsessionid=58255EF78BEDCF73175AB6B9D86D0C55.

# Appendix I: Crime Data Sources

## United States

AH Datalytics (www.ahdatalytics.com/dashboards/ytd-murder-comparison/).

Council on Criminal Justice (https://counciloncj.org/category/crime-trends/).

Gun Violence Archive (www.gunviolencearchive.org/methodology).

National Crime Victimization Survey (https://bjs.ojp.gov/data-collection/ncvs).

National Incident-Based Reporting System (www.fbi.gov/how-we-can-help-you/need-an-fbi-service-or-more-information/ucr/nibrs).

National Violent Death Reporting System (www.cdc.gov/violenceprevention/datasources/nvdrs/index.html).

National Vital Statistics System Fatal Injury Reports (www.cdc.gov/injury/wisqars/fatal.html).

Supplementary Homicide Reports (www.ojjdp.gov/ojstatbb/ezashr/).

Uniform Crime Reports (www.fbi.gov/how-we-can-help-you/need-an-fbi-service-or-more-information/ucr/publications).

## International

European Sourcebook of Crime and Criminal Justice Statistics (https://wp.unil.ch/europeansourcebook/).

International Crime Victimization Survey (www.icpsr.umich.edu/web/ICPSR/series/175).

United Nations Surveys on Crime Trends and the Operations of Criminal Justice Systems (www.unodc.org/unodc/en/data-and-analysis/United-Nations-Surveys-on-Crime-Trends-and-the-Operations-of-Criminal-Justice-Systems.html).

World Health Organization (www.who.int/data/gho/data/indicators/indicator-details/GHO/estimates-of-rates-of-homicides-per-100-000-population).

# Appendix II: Forecasting Methods and Models

## Testing the Crime Series for Stationarity

A cursory glance at Figure 11 indicates that New York's violent and property crime rates between 1980 and 2016 are nonstationary. Neither series exhibits a constant mean over time. This perception is supported by formal tests to determine whether the two time series contain a unit root (i.e., are nonstationary). Both the augmented Dickey–Fuller (ADF) test and the Phillips–Perron (PP) test failed to reject the null hypothesis of a unit root for both series.[30] New York's violent and property crime rates between 1980 and 2016 are nonstationary and conform to a random walk.

The two series were therefore converted to first differences, and the same tests were conducted. The PP test rejected the null hypothesis that the first-differenced violent and property crime series contain a unit root at the conventional 5% level of significance (p=.03 for both series). When converted to first differences both series are stationary.

## ARIMA Models and Forecasting Results

ARIMA models estimate the autoregressive (denoted $p$), differencing (denoted $d$), and moving average (denoted $q$) properties of a time series. Several multivariate ARIMA$_{(p,d,q)}$ models were estimated on the New York first-differenced crime rates from 1980 to 2016. The models that minimized the mean-squared errors and mean absolute errors of the estimates for both the estimation period (1980–2016) and validation period (2017–2021) of the time series were retained. These models were then used to forecast the violent and property crime rates for 2022 to 2024. Univariate ARIMA models were also used to forecast unobserved income and imprisonment values for these years.[31] The multivariate ARIMA models include the income-adjusted inflation rate and the one-year lagged imprisonment rate.

In Table A-1 the year-to-year forecasted changes in New York's violent and property crime rate are added to the previous year's rates to generate forecasts of the current year's rates during the validation period. The best-fitting forecast model for violent crime is an ARIMA$_{(2,0,2)}$ model, which contains two

---

[30] The p-value for the augmented Dickey-Fuller test statistic $Z_{(t)}$ is .88 and is .82 for the Phillips–Perron test. Including a trend in the two series does not alter these results.

[31] The best fitting models for median household income and imprisonment are, respectively, ARIMA$_{(2,2,2)}$, and ARIMA$_{(2,0,2)}$ with a constant.

**Table A-1** Forecasts of New York violent and property crime rates, 2017–2024.

| | Violent Crime (ARIMA$_{(2,0,2)}$) | | | Property Crime (ARIMA$_{(0,2,0)}$) | | |
|---|---|---|---|---|---|---|
| | Observed Rate | Forecasted Rate | Percentage Error | Observed Rate | Forecasted Rate | Percentage Error |
| 2017 | 538.5 | 576.9 | 7.13% | 1447.5 | 1513.6 | 4.57% |
| 2018 | 549.0 | 503.4 | −8.32% | 1524.6 | 1490.3 | −2.25% |
| 2019 | 573.6 | 542.8 | −5.38% | 1467.0 | 1500.3 | 2.27% |
| 2020 | 546.7 | 585.0 | 7.00% | 1474.5 | 1455.8 | −1.27% |
| 2021 | 630.2 | 521.4 | −17.26% | 1572.4 | 1467.0 | −6.71% |
| | | | | | | |
| MAPE[1] | | | 9.02% | | | 3.41% |
| Mean | 567.6 | 545.9 | −3.82% | 1497.2 | 1485.4 | −.79% |
| | | | | | | |
| 2022 | | 699.1 | | | 1696.0 | |
| 2023 | | 757.9 | | | 1840.4 | |
| 2024 | | 768.2 | | | 1774.5 | |

[1] MAPE= Mean absolute percentage error

autoregressive terms and first- and second-order moving average terms. The model forecasts a violent crime rate in 2017 of about 577 violent crimes per 100,000 population, which is about 7% above the observed rate of 538. The forecasted rates fall below the observed rates by about 8% and 5% in 2018 and 2019 and 7% above the observed rate in 2020. In 2021 the forecasted violent crime rate of 521 violent crimes per 100,000 is about 17% below the observed rate of 630. The mean absolute percentage error (MAPE) during the five-year validation period indicates that, on average, the forecasted violent crime rate diverges in either direction from the observed rate by about 9%.

The best-fitting forecast model for property crime is an $ARIMA_{(0,2,0)}$ model that contains first- and second-difference terms in addition to the substantive covariates. None of the forecasted property crime rates diverges from the observed rates by more than 7% during the validation period, and the average divergence is just 3.4%. The subsequent forecasts indicate a sizable rise in New York's property crime rate in 2022 and a smaller rise in 2023, before falling in 2024.

# References

Adler, Freda. 1975. Sisters in Crime. New York: McGraw-Hill. Agnew, Robert. 2005. Pressured into Crime: An Overview of General Strain Theory. New York: Oxford

Arvanites, Thomas M., and Robert H. Defina. 2006. Business cycles and street crime. Criminology 44: 139–164.

Azrael, Deborah, Philip J. Cook, and Matthew Miller. 2004. State and local prevalence of firearms ownership. Journal of Quantitative Criminology 20: 43–62.

Banerjee, Anindya, Stephen G. Hall, Georgios P. Kouretas, and George S. Tavlas. 2023. Advances in forecasting: An introduction in light of the debate on inflation forecasting. Journal of Forecasting 42: 455–463.

Baumer, Eric P. 2008. An empirical assessment of the contemporary crime trends puzzle: A modest step toward a more comprehensive agenda. In Understanding Crime Trends, edited by Arthur S. Goldberger and Richard Rosenfeld. Washington, DC: National Academies Press, 127–176.

Baumer, Eric P., and Kevin T. Wolff. 2014. Evaluating contemporary crime drop(s) in America, New York City, and many other places. Justice Quarterly 31: 5–38.

Baumer, Eric P., Maria Velez, and Richard Rosenfeld. 2018. Understanding contemporary crime trends: A critical assessment of existing research and a blueprint for future inquiry. Annual Review of Criminology 1: 195–217.

Becker, Gary. 1968. Crime and punishment: an economic approach. Journal of Political Economy 73: 169–217.

Black, Donald. 1983. Crime as social control. American Sociological Review 48: 34–45.

Blau, Judith R., and Peter M. Blau. 1982. The cost of inequality: Metropolitan structure and violent crime. American Sociological Review 47: 114–129.

Blumstein, Alfred. 1995. Youth violence, guns, and the illicit-drug industry. Journal of Criminal Law and Criminology 86: 10–36.

Blumstein, Alfred, and Joel Wallman. 2000. The Crime Drop in America. New York: Cambridge University Press

Box, George E. P., Gwilym M. Jenkins, Gregory C. Reinsel, and Greta M. Ljung. 2016. Time Series Analysis: Forecasting and Control. 5th ed. Hoboken, NJ: Wiley.

Braga, Anthony A., Martin A. Andresen, and Brian Lawton. 2017. The law of crime concentration at places: Editors' introduction. Journal of Quantitative Criminology 33: 421–426.

Braga, Anthony A., Elizabeth Griffiths, Keller Sheppard, and Stephen Douglas. 2021. Firearm instrumentality: Do guns make violent situations more lethal? Annual Review of Criminology 4: 147–164.

Braithwaite, John. 2022. Macrocriminology and Freedom. Canberra, Australia: Australian National University Press.

Breault, Kevin D., and Augustine J. Kposowa. 1997. The effects of marital status on adult female homicides in the United States. Journal of Quantitative Criminology 13: 217–230.

Brockwell, Peter J., and Richard A. Davis. 2016. Introduction to Time Series and Forecasting. 3rd ed. Hague: Springer.

Browne, Angela, and Kirk R. Williams. 1989. Exploring the effect of resource availability and the likelihood of female-perpetrated homicides. Law & Society Review 23: 75–94.

Browne, Angela, and Kirk R. Williams. 1993. Gender, intimacy, and lethal violence: Trends from 1976 through 1987. Gender & Society 7: 78–98.

Browne, Angela, Kirk R. Williams, and Donald G. Dutton. 1999. Homicide between intimate partners. In Homicide: A Sourcebook of Social Research, edited by M. Duane Smith and Margaret A. Zahn. Thousand Oaks, CA: Sage, 149–164.

Bushway, Shawn D. 2011. Labor markets and crime. In Crime and Public Policy, edited by James Q. Wilson and Joan Petersilia. New York: Oxford University Press, 183–209.

Bushway, Shawn, Philip J. Cook, and Matthew Phillips. 2013. The net effect of the business cycle on crime and violence. In Economics and Youth Violence: Crime Disadvantage, and Community, edited by Richard Rosenfeld, Mark Edberg, Xiangming Fang, and Curtis S. Florence. New York: New York University Press.

Campbell, Jacquelyn C., Nancy Glass, Phyllis W. Sharps, Kathryn Laughon, and Tina Bloom. 2007. Intimate partner homicide: Review and implications of research and policy. Trauma, Violence, & Abuse 8: 246–269.

Cantor, David, and Kenneth C. Land. 1985. Unemployment and crime rates in the Post-World War II United States: A theoretical and empirical analysis. American Sociological Review 50: 317–332.

Cassell, Paul G. 2020. Explaining the recent homicide spikes in US cities: The "Minneapolis Effect" and the decline in proactive policing. Federal Sentencing Reporter 33: 83–127.

Chiricos, Theodore G. 1987. Rates of crime and unemployment: An analysis of aggregate research evidence. Social Problems 34: 187–212.

Clear, Todd R. 2007. Imprisoning Communities: How Mass Incarceration Makes Disadvantaged Neighborhoods Worse. New York: Oxford University Press.

Cohen, Lawrence E., and Marcus Felson. 1979. Social change and crime rate trends: A routine activity approach. American Sociological Review 44: 588–608.

Cohen, Lawrence E., and Kenneth C. Land. 1987. Age structure and crime: Symmetry versus asymmetry and the projection of crime rates through the 1990s. American Sociological Review, 52, 170–183.

Cohen, Lawrence E., Marcus Felson, and Kenneth C. Land. 1980. Property crime rates in the United States – A macro macrodynamic analysis, 1947–1977 – with ex ante forecasts for the mid-1980s. American Journal of Sociology 86: 90–118.

Cook, Philip J., and John H. Laub. 1998. The unprecedented epidemic in youth violence. Crime and Justice 24: 27–64.

Cook, Philip J., and Gary A. Zarkin. 1985. Crime and the business cycle. Journal of Legal Studies 14: 115–128.

Cornish, Derek, and Clarke, Ronald V. 1986. The Reasoning Criminal: Rational Choice Perspectives on Offending. Hague: Springer.

Coyne-Beasley Tamera, Kara S. McGee, Renee M. Johnson, and Clayton Bordley. 2002. The association of handgun ownership and storage practices with safety consciousness. Archives of Pediatric & Adolescent Medicine 156: 763–768.

DiIullio, John. 1995. The coming of the super-predator. Weekly Standard (November 27). www.washingtonexaminer.com/weekly-standard/the-coming-of-the-super-predators.

Dobrin, Adam. 2001. The risk of offending on homicide victimization: A case control study. Journal of Research in Crime and Delinquency 38: 154–173.

Donnelly, Kevin. 2016. Adolphe Quetelet, Social Physics and the Average Men of Science, 1796–1874. New York: Routledge.

Donohue, John J., and Steven Levitt. 2001. The impact of legalized abortion on crime. Quarterly Journal of Economics 116: 379–420.

Donohue, John J., and Steven Levitt. 2020. The impact of legalized abortion on crime over the last two decades. American Law and Economics Review 22: 241–302.

DuBois, W. E. B. (1996 [1899]). The Philadelphia Negro: A Social Study. Philadelphia: University of Pennsylvania Press.

Dugan, Laura, Daniel S. Nagin, and Richard Rosenfeld. 1999. Explaining the decline in intimate partner homicide: The effects of changing domesticity, women's status, and domestic violence resources. Homicide Studies 3: 187–214.

Dugan, Laura, Daniel S. Nagin, and Richard Rosenfeld. 2003. Exposure reduction or retaliation? The effects of domestic violence resources on intimate-partner homicide. Law & Society Review 37: 169–198.

Duggan, Mark. 2001. More guns, more crime. Journal of Political Economy 109: 1086–1114.

Durkheim, Emile. 1951 [1897]. Suicide: A Study in Sociology. Glencoe, Il: Free Press.

Durkheim, Emile. 1966 [1895]. The Rules of the Sociological Method. New York: Free Press.

Easterlin, Richard A. 1980. Birth and Fortune: The Impact of Numbers on Personal Welfare. New York: Basic Books.

Eisner, Manuel. 2001. Modernization, self-control, and lethal violence: The long-term dynamics of European homicide rates in theoretical perspective. British Journal of Criminology 41: 618–638.

Elias, Norbert. 1978 [1939]. The Civilizing Process: The History of Manners and State Formation and Civilization. Oxford: Blackwell.

Ehrlich, Isaac. 1973. Participation in illegitimate activities: A theoretical and empirical investigation. Journal of Political Economy 81: 521–565.

Feld, Scott, and Shawn Bauldry. 2018. Separate, unequal, and uncorrelated: Why we need to consider race-specific homicide rates in US metropolitan areas. Socius 4: 1–8.

Feldmeyer, Ben, Diana Sun, Casey T. Harris, and Francis T. Cullen. 2022. More immigrants, less death: An analysis of immigration effects on county-level drug overdose deaths, 2000–2015. Criminology 60: 667–699.

Felson, Marcus K. 2002. Crime and Everyday Life. Thousand Oaks, CA: Sage.

Fox, James A. 1978. Forecasting Crime Data: An Econometric Analysis. New York: Lexington Books.

Fox, James A., and Alex R. Piquero. 2003. Deadly demographics: Population characteristics and forecasting homicide trends. Crime & Delinquency 49: 339–359.

Fox, James A., and Marc L. Swatt. 2009. Multiple imputation of the supplementary homicide reports, 1976–2005. Journal of Quantitative Criminology 25: 51–77.

Fridel, Emma E., and James Alan Fox. 2019. Gender differences in patterns and trends in U.S. homicide, 1976–2017. Violence and Gender 6: 27–36.

Garland, David. 1990. Punishment and Modern Society: A Study in Social Theory. Chicago: University of Chicago Press.

Garland, David. 2001. The Culture of Control: Crime and Social Order in Contemporary Society. Chicago: University of Chicago Press.

Gaston, Shytierra, Jamein P. Cunningham, and Rob Gillezeau. 2019. A Ferguson Effect, the drug epidemic, both, or neither? Explaining the 2015 and 2016 U.S. homicide rises by race and ethnicity. Homicide Studies 23: 285–313.

Gill, Charlotte, Alese Wooditch, and David Weisburd. 2017. Testing the law of crime concentration at place in a suburban setting: Implications for research and practice. Journal of Quantitative Criminology 33: 519–545.

Gorr, Wilpen, Andreas Olligschlaeger, and Yvonne Thompson. 2003. Short-term forecasting of crime. International Journal of Forecasting 19: 579–594.

Gottfredson, Michael R., and Travis Hirschi. 1990. A General Theory of Crime. Stanford, CA: Stanford University Press.

Gould, Eric D., Bruce A. Weinberg, and David B. Mustard. 2002. Crime rates and local labor market opportunities in the United States: 1979–1997. Review of Economics and Statistics 84: 45–61.

Greenberg, David F., and Nancy J. Larkin. 1985. Age-cohort analysis of arrest rates. Journal of Quantitative Criminology 1: 227–40.

Grogger, Jeffrey T. 1998. Market wages and youth crime. Journal of Labor Economics 16: 756–791.

Haberman, Clyde. 2014. When youth violence spurred "superpredator" fear. New York Times (April 6). www.nytimes.com/2014/04/07/us/politics/killing-on-bus-recalls-superpredator-threat-of-90s.html.

Hagan, John, Bill McCarthy, and Daniel Herda. 2020. What the study of legal cynicism and crime can tell us about reliability, validity, and versatility in law and social science research. Annual Review of Law and Social Science 16: 1–20.

Harris, Casey T., and Ben Feldmeyer. 2013. Latino immigration and White, Black, and Latino violent crime: A comparison of traditional and non-traditional immigrant destinations. Social Science Quarterly 42: 202–216.

Hepburn, Lisa M., and David Hemenway. 2004. Firearm availability and homicide: A review of the literature. Aggression and Violent Behavior 9: 417–440.

Hindelang, Michael J., Michael R. Gottfredson, and James Garofalo. 1978. Victims of Personal Crime: An Empirical Foundation for a Theory of Personal Victimization. Cambridge, MA: Ballinger.

Hipp, John R., and Xiaoshuang Iris Luo. 2022. Improving or declining: What are the consequences for changes in local crime? Criminology 60: 480–507 https://doi.org/10.1111/1745-9125.12309.

Hirschi, Travis. 1969. Causes of Delinquency. Berkeley, CA: University of California Press.

Hirschi, Travis, and Michael Gottfredson. 1983. Age and the explanation of crime. American Journal of Sociology 89: 552–584.

Hyndman, Rob J., and George Athanasopoulos. 2018. Forecasting: Principles and Practice. 2nd ed. Otexts.

Johnson, Ryan S., Shawn Kantor, and Price V. Fishback. 2007. Striking at the roots of crime: The impact of social welfare spending on crime during the Great Depression. National Bureau of Economic Research Working Paper No. 12825 (January).

Johnson, Rucker, and Steven Raphael. 2012. How much crime reduction does the marginal prisoner buy? Journal of Law and Economics 55: 275–310.

Joyce, Ted. 2009. A simple test of abortion and crime. Review of Economics and Statistics 91: 112–123.

Karstedt, Susanne. 2010. The new institutionalism in criminology: Approaches, theories, and themes. In The Sage Handbook of Criminological Theory, edited by Eugene McLaughlin and Tim Newburn. London: Sage, 337–359.

Kena, Grace, and Rachel E. Morgan. 2023. Criminal Victimization in the 22 Largest U.S. States, 2017–2019. Washington, DC: U.S. Department of Justice. https://bjs.ojp.gov/library/publications/criminal-victimization-22-largest-us-states-2017-2019#additional-details-0.

Kim, Jaeok, Shawn Bushway, and Hui-Shien Tsao. 2016. Identifying classes of explanations for crime drop: Period and cohort effects for New York state. Journal of Quantitative Criminology 32: 357–375.

Kirk, David S., and Andrew V. Papachristos. 2015. Concentrated disadvantage, the persistence of legal cynicism, and crime: Revisiting the conception of "culture" in criminology. In Challenging Criminological Theory: The Legacy of Ruth Rosner Kornhauser, edited by Francis T. Cullen, Pamela Wilcox, Robert J. Sampson, and Brendan D. Dooley. New York: Routledge.

Kleck, Gary, and Karen McElrath. 1991. The effects of weaponry on human violence. Social Forces 69: 669–692.

Kornhauser, Ruth. 1978. Social Sources of Delinquency: An Appraisal of Analytic Models. Chicago: University of Chicago Press.

LaFree, Gary. 1998. Losing Legitimacy: Street Crime and the Decline of Social Institutions in America. Boulder, CO: Westview.

LaFree, Gary, Eric P. Baumer, and Robert O'Brien. 2010. Still separate and unequal?: A city-level analysis of the Black-White gap in homicide arrests since 1960. American Sociological Review 75: 75–100.

Land, Kenneth C., and Patricia L. McCall. 2001. The indeterminacy of forecasts of crime rates and juvenile offenses. Appendix B in Institute of Medicine,

Juvenile Crime, Juvenile Justice. Washington, DC: National Academies Press.

Land, Kenneth C., Patricia L. McCall, and Lawrence E. Cohen. 1990. Structural covariates of homicide rates: Are there any invariances across time and social space? American Journal of Sociology 95: 922–963.

Lau, Tim. 2020. Predictive Policing Explained. Brennan Center for Justice www.brennancenter.org/our-work/research-reports/predictive-policing-explained.

Lauritsen, Janet L. (2023). The future of crime data: 2022 American Society of Criminology presidential address. Criminology 61:187–203.

Lauritsen, Janet L., and Karen Heimer. 2008. The gender gap in violent victimization, 1973–2004. Journal of Quantitative Criminology 24: 125–147.

Lauritsen, Janet L., and Karen Heimer. 2010. Violent victimization among males and economic conditions. Criminology & Public Policy 9: 665–692.

Lauritsen, Janet L. Karen Heimer, and Joseph B. Lang. 2018. The enduring significance of racial and ethnic disparities in male violent victimization, 1973–2010. Du Bois Review: Social Science Research on Race 15: 69–87.

Lauritsen, Janet L. Karen Heimer, and Joseph B. Lang. 2022. The Disappearing Gender Gap in Violent Victimization. Seminar Paper Presented at the University of Maryland, College Park, MD.

Lauritsen, Janet L., Karen Heimer, and James P. Lynch. 2009. Trends in the gender gap in violent offending: New evidence from the National Crime Victimization Survey. Criminology 47: 361–399.

Lauritsen, Janet, Maribeth Rezey, and Karen Heimer. 2016. When choice of data matters: Analyses of U.S. crime trends, 1973–2012. Journal of Quantitative Criminology 32: 335–355.

Lee, Matthew R., William B. Bankston, Timothy C. Hayes, and Shaun A. Thomas. 2007. Revisiting the southern subculture of violence. Sociological Quarterly 48: 253–275.

Levitt, Steven D. 1996. The effect of prison population size on crime rates: Evidence from prison overcrowding legislation. Quarterly Journal of Economics 111: 319–352.

Lichter, Daniel T., and Kenneth M. Johnson. 2009. Immigrant gateways and Hispanic migration to new destinations. International Migration Review 43: 496–518.

Light, Michael T. 2017. Re-examining the relationship between Latino immigration and racial/ethnic violence. Social Science Research 65: 222–239.

Light, Michael T., and Julia T. Thomas. 2019. Segregation and violence reconsidered: Do Whites benefit from residential segregation? American Sociological Review 84: 690–725.

Light, Michael T., and Jeffery T. Ulmer. 2016. Explaining the gaps in White, Black, and Hispanic violence since 1990: Accounting for immigration, incarceration, and inequality. American Sociological Review 81: 290–315.

Lo, Celia C., Rebecca J. Howell, and Tyrone C. Cheng. 2012. Explaining Black-White differences in homicide victimization. Aggression and Violent Behavior 18: 125–134.

Loftin, Colin. 1986. Assaultive violence as a contagious social process. Bulletin of the New York Academy of Medicine 62: 550–555.

Lopez, Ernesto, and Richard Rosenfeld. 2021. Crime, quarantine, and the U.S. coronavirus pandemic. Criminology & Public Policy 20: 401–422.

Lott, John R., Jr. 1998. More Guns, Less Crime. Chicago: University of Chicago Press.

Lott, John R., Jr. 2010. More Guns, Less Crime. 3rd ed. Chicago: University of Chicago Press.

Lu, Yunmei, Liying Luo, and Mateus R. Santos. 2022. Social change and race-specific homicide trajectories: An age-period-cohort analysis. Journal of Research in Crime and Delinquency. https://doi.org/10.1177/00224278221129886.

Ludwig-Dehm, Sarah, and John Iceland. 2017. Hispanic concentrated poverty in traditional and new destinations, 2010–2014. Population Research Policy Review 36: 833–850.

Lum, Cynthia, Carl Maupin, and Megan Stoltz. 2022. The supply and demand shifts in policing at the start of the pandemic: A national multi-wave survey of the impacts of COVID-19 on American law enforcement. Police Quarterly 26:495–519. https://doi.org/10.1177/10986111221148217.

Lynch, James P., and Lynn A. Addington. 2007. Understanding Crime Statistics: Revisiting the Divergence of the NCVS and UCR. New York: Cambridge University Press.

Mac Donald, Heather. 2016. The War on Cops. New York: Encounter Books.

Maltz, Michael D., and Joseph Targonski. 2002. A note on the use of county-level UCR data. Journal of Quantitative Criminology 18: 297–318.

Martinez, Ramiro, Jr. 2002. Latino homicide: Immigration, Violence, and Community. New York: Routledge.

Martinez, Ramiro, Jr. , and Matthew T. Lee. 2000. On immigration and crime. Criminal Justice 1: 486–524.

Massey, Douglas S. 1995. Getting away with murder: Segregation and violent crime in urban America. University of Pennsylvania Law Review 143: 1203–1232.

McCall, Patricia L., Kenneth C. Land, and Karen F. Parker. 2010. An empirical assessment of what we know about structural covariates of homicide rates: A return to a classic 20 years later. Homicide Studies 14: 219–243.

McDowall, David, and Colin Loftin. 2009. Do US city crime rates follow a national trend? The influence of nationwide conditions on local crime patterns. Journal of Quantitative Criminology 25: 307–324.

McNulty, Thomas L. 2001. Assessing the race-violence relationship at the macro level: The assumption of racial invariance and the problem of restricted distributions. Criminology 39: 467–490.

Merton, Robert K. 1938. Social structure and anomie. American Sociological Review 38: 672–682.

Messner, Steven F., and Richard Rosenfeld. 1999. Social structure and homicide: Theory and research. In Homicide Studies: A Sourcebook of Social Research, edited by M. Duane Smith and Margaret Zahn. Thousand Oaks, CA: Sage.

Messner, Steven F., and Richard Rosenfeld. 2013. Crime and the American Dream, 5th ed. Boston, MA: Cengage.

Messner, Steven F., Richard Rosenfeld, and Susanne Karstedt. 2011. Social institutions and crime. In Oxford Handbook of Criminological Theory, edited by Francis T. Cullen and Pamela Wilcox. New York: Oxford University Press, 405–423.

Morgan, Rachel, and Alexandra Thompson. 2021. Criminal Victimization, 2020. Washington, DC: US Department of Justice. https://bjs.ojp.gov/sites/g/files/xyckuh236/files/media/document/cv20.pdf.

Morgan, Rachel, and Alexandra Thompson. 2022. The Nation's Two Crime Measures, 2011–2020. Washington, DC: US Department of Justice. https://bjs.ojp.gov/content/pub/pdf/ntcm1120.pdf.

Morin, Rich, Kim Parker, Renee Stepler, and Andrew Mercer. 2017. Behind the Badge. Pew Research Center. www.pewresearch.org/social-trends/2017/01/11/behind-the-badge/.

Nagin, Daniel S. 2005. Group-Based Modeling of Development. Cambridge, MA: Harvard University Press.

National Research Council. 2005. Firearms and Violence: A Critical Review. Washington, DC: The National Academies Press.

National Research Council. 2014. The Growth of Incarceration in the United States: Exploring Causes and Consequences. Washington, DC: National Academies Press.

Nolan, James J., Stephen M. Haas, and Jessica S. Napier. 2011. Estimating the impact of classification error on the "statistical accuracy" of uniform crime reports. Journal of Quantitative Criminology 27: 497–519.

O'Brien, Robert M., and Jean Stockard. 2009. Can cohort replacement explain changes in the relationship between age and homicide offending? Journal of Quantitative Criminology 25: 79–101.

O'Carroll, Patrick W., and James A. Mercy. 1989. Regional variation in homicide rates: Why is the West so violent? Violence and Victims 4: 17–25.

O'Flaherty, Brendan, and Rajiv Sethi. 2010. Homicide in black and white. Journal of Urban Economics 68: 215–230.

Ousey, Graham C. 1999. Homicide, structural factors, and the racial invariance assumption. Criminology 37: 405–426.

Ousey, Graham C., and Charis E. Kubrin. 2018. Immigration and crime: Assessing a contentious issue. Annual Review of Criminology 1: 63–84.

Parker, Robert N. 1995. Alcohol and Homicide. Albany, NY: SUNY Press.

Parker, Robert Nash, and Kathleen Auerhahn. 1998. Alcohol, drugs, and violence. Annual Review of Sociology 24: 291–311.

Pepper, John V. 2008. Forecasting crime: A city-level analysis. In Understanding Crime Trends, edited by Arthur S. Goldberger and Richard Rosenfeld. Washington, DC: National Academies Press, 177–210.

Peterson, Ruth D., and Lauren J. Krivo. 2010. Divergent Social Worlds: Neighborhood Crime and the Racial-Spatial Divide. New York: Russell Sage.

Phillips, Julie A. 2002. White, Black, and Latino homicide rates: Why the difference? Social Problems 49: 349–373.

Phillips, Julie A. 2006. The relationship between age structure and homicide rates in the United States, 1970 to 1999. Journal of Research in Crime and Delinquency 43: 230–260.

Pinker, Steven. 2012. The Better Angels of Our Nature: A History of Violence and Humanity. London: Penguin.

Pridemore, William Alex, and Sang-Weon Kim. 2006. Democratization and political change as threats to collective sentiments: Testing Durkheim in Russia. The ANNALS of the American Academy of Political and Social Science 605: 82–103.

Carole A., Puzone, Saltzman, Linda A., Kresnow, Marcy-Jo, Thompson, Martie P., and Mercy, James A. 2000. National trends in intimate partner homicide: United States, 1976-1995. Violence Against Women 6: 409–426.

RAND. 2018. The Relationship Between Firearm Prevalence and Violent Crime (March 2). www.rand.org/research/gun-policy/analysis/essays/firearm-prevalence-violent-crime.html.

Raphael, Steven, and Rudolf Winter-Ebmer. 2001. Identifying the effect unemployment on crime. Journal of Law and Economics 44: 259–283.

Reuter, Peter. 2009. Systemic violence in drug markets. Crime, Law, and Social Change 52: 275-284.

Reuter, Peter, ed. 2010. Understanding the Demand for Illegal Drugs. Washington, DC: National Academies Press.

Reyes, Jessica Wolpaw. 2007. Environmental policy as social policy? The impact of childhood lead exposure on crime. The B.E. Journal of Economic Analysis & Policy 7. https://doi.org/10.2202/1935-1682.1796.

Rogers, Ethan M., Mark T. Berg, and Richard Rosenfeld. 2022. A tale of three homicide booms in the U.S. Presented at the annual meeting of the American Society of Criminology, Atlanta, GA.

Rosenfeld, Richard. 1997. Changing relationships between men and women: A note on the decline in intimate partner homicide. Homicide Studies 1: 72–83.

Rosenfeld, Richard. 2000. Patterns in adult homicide: 1980–1995. In The Crime Drop in America, edited by Alfred Blumstein and Joel Wallman. New York: Cambridge University Press.

Rosenfeld, Richard. 2009. Crime is the problem: Homicide, acquisitive crime, and economic conditions. Journal of Quantitative Criminology 25: 287–306.

Rosenfeld, Richard. 2011. Changing crime rates. In Crime and Public Policy, edited by James Q. Wilson and Joan Petersilia. New York: Oxford University Press, 559–588.

Rosenfeld, Richard. 2018. Studying crime trends: Normal science and exogenous shocks. The 2017 Sutherland Address. Criminology 56: 5–26.

Rosenfeld, Richard, and Mark Berg. 2023. Forecasting future crime rates. Journal of Contemporary Criminal Justice. https://doi.org/10.1177/10439862231190215.

Rosenfeld, Richard, and Robert Fornango. 2007. The impact of economic conditions on robbery and property crime: The role of consumer sentiment. Criminology 45: 735–769.

Rosenfeld, Richard, and Aaron Levin. 2016. Acquisitive crime and inflation in the United States: 1960–2012. Journal of Quantitative Criminology 32: 427–447.

Rosenfeld, Richard, and Ernesto Lopez. 2022. Pandemic, Social Unrest, and Crime in U.S. Cities: Year-End 2021 Update. Washington, DC: Council on Criminal Justice.

Rosenfeld, Richard, and Steven F. Messner. 2009. The crime drop in comparative perspective: The impact of the economy and imprisonment on American and European burglary rates. British Journal of Sociology 60: 445–471.

Rosenfeld, Richard, and Steven F. Messner. 2013. Crime and the Economy. Thousand Oaks, CA: Sage.

Rosenfeld, Richard, and Matt Vogel. 2023. Homicide, acquisitive crime, and inflation: A city-level longitudinal analysis. Crime & Delinquency 69: 3–33.

Rosenfeld, Richard, Randolph Roth, and Joel Wallman. 2021a. Homicide and the opioid epidemic: A longitudinal analysis. Homicide Studies 27: 321–337 https://doi.org/10.1177/10887679211054418.

Rosenfeld, Richard, Matt Vogel, and Timothy McCuddy. 2019. Crime and inflation in U.S. cities. Journal of Quantitative Criminology 35: 195–210.

Rosenfeld, Richard, Joel Wallman, and Randolph Roth. 2021. The opioid epidemic and homicide in the United States. Journal of Research in Crime and Delinquency 58: 545–590.

Rosenfeld, Richard, Shytierra Gaston, Howard Spivak, and Seri Irazola. 2017. Assessing and Responding to the Recent Homicide Rise in the United States. NCJ 251067. Washington, DC: National Institute of Justice.

Roth, Randolph. 2009. American Homicide. Cambridge, MA: Harvard University Press.

Sagi, Phillip C., and Charles F. Wellford. 1968. Age composition and patterns of change in crime statistics. Journal of Criminal Law, Criminology and Police Science, 59: 29–36.

Sampson, Robert J. 2008. Rethinking crime and immigration. Contexts 7: 28–33.

Sampson, Robert J., and Dawn Jeglum Bartusch. 1998. Legal cynicism and (subcultural?) tolerance of deviance: The neighborhood context of racial differences. Law & Society Review 32: 777–804.

Sampson, Robert J., and William Julius Wilson. 1995. Toward a theory of race. crime, and urban inequality. In Crime and Inequality, edited by John Hagan and Ruth D. Peterson. Stanford, CA: Stanford University Press, 37–54.

Sampson, Robert J., William Julius Wilson, and Hanna Katz. 2018. Reassessing "Toward a theory of race, crime, and urban inequality": Enduring and new challenges in 21st century America. Du Bois Review 15: 13–34.

Schuster, Larry. 1995. "Bloodbath" predicted as children age. United Press International (February 17). www.upi.com/Archives/1995/02/17/Bloodbath-predicted-as-children-age/7792792997200/.

Shelley, Louise I. 1981. Crime and Modernization: The Impact of Industrialization and Urbanization on Crime. Carbondale, IL: Southern Illinois University Press.

Shihadeh, Edward S., and Raymond E. Barranco. 2013. The imperative of place: Homicide and the new Latino migration. Sociological Quarterly 54: 81–104.

Shiller, Robert J. 1997. Why do people dislike inflation? In Reducing Inflation: Motivation and Strategy, edited by Christina D. Romer and David H. Romer. Chicago: University of Chicago Press, 13–70.

Simon, Rita James. 1975. Women and Crime. Lexington, MA: Lexington Books.

Spelman, William. 2022. How cohorts changed crime rates, 1980–2016. Journal of Quantitative Criminology 38: 637–671.

Steffensmeier, Darrell. 1980. Sex differences in patterns of adult crime, 1965-77: A review and assessment. Social Forces 58: 1080–1108.

Steffensmeier, Darrell J., and Miles D. Harer. 1987. Is the crime rate really falling? An "aging" U.S. population and its Impact on the nation's crime rate, 1980–84. Journal of Research in Crime and Delinquency 24: 23–48.

Steffensmeier, Darrell, Cathy Streifel, and Miles D. Harer. 1987. Relative cohort size and youth crime in the United States, 1953–1984. American Sociological Review 52: 702–710.

Steffensmeier, Darrell, Jeffrey T. Ulmer, Ben Feldmeyer, and Casey T. Harris. 2010. Scope and conceptual issues in testing the race-crime invariance thesis: Black, White, and Hispanic comparisons. Criminology 48: 1133–1169.

Stevenson, Betsey, and Justin Wolfers. 2006. Bargaining in the shadow of the law: Divorce laws and family distress. Quarterly Journal of Economics 121: 267–288.

Sweeten, Gary, Alex R. Piquero, and Laurence Steinberg. 2013. Age and the explanation of crime, revisited. Journal of Youth and Adolescence 42: 921–938.

Thomas, Dorothy Swaine. 1927. Social Aspects of the Business Cycle. New York: Knopf.

Tsay, Ruey S. 2010. Analysis of Financial Time Series. 3rd ed. Chicago: University of Chicago Press.

Tyler, Tom R. 1990. Why People Obey the Law. New Haven, CT: Yale University Press.

Tyler, Tom R., Phillip Atiba Goff, and Robert J. MacCoun. 2015. The impact of psychological science on policing in the United States: Procedural justice, legitimacy, and effective law enforcement. Psychological Science in the Public Interest 16: 75–109.

Ulmer, Jeffrey T., Casey T. Harris, and Darrell Steffensmeier. 2012. Racial and ethnic disparities in structural disadvantage and crime: White, Black, and Hispanic comparisons. Social Science Quarterly 93: 799–819.

Van Dijk, Jan, Paul Nieuwbeerta, and Jacqueline Joudo Larsen. 2022. Global crime patterns: An analysis of survey data from 166 countries around the world, 2006–2019. Journal of Quantitative Criminology 38: 793–827.

Velez, Maria B., Lauren J. Krivo, and Ruth D. Peterson. 2003. Structural inequality and homicide: An assessment of the Black-White gap in killings. Criminology 41: 645–672.

Waters, Malcolm. 1996. Daniel Bell. New York: Routledge.

Weisburd, David. 2015. The law of crime concentration and the criminology of place. Criminology 53: 133–157.

Weisburd, David, Elizabeth R. Groff, and Sue-Ming Yang. 2012. The criminology of place: street segments and our understanding of the crime problem. New York: Oxford University Press.

Weisburd, David, Shawn Bushway, Cynthia Lum, and Sue-Ming Yang. 2004. Trajectories of crime at places: A longitudinal study of street segments in the city of Seattle. Criminology 42: 283–322.

White, Clair, David Weisburd, and Sean Wire. 2018. Examining the impact of the Freddie Gray unrest on perceptions of the police. Criminology & Public Policy 17: 829–858.

Whitt, Hugh P., and Victor W. Reinking. 2002. A Translation of André-Michel Guerry's Essay on the Moral Statistics of France (1833): A Sociological Report to the French Academy of Science. Lewiston, NY: Edwin Mellen Press.

Wilson, James Q. 1985. Thinking About Crime. Revised ed. New York: Knopf.

Wilson, James Q. 2011. Hard times, fewer crimes. Wall Street Journal (May 28). www.wsj.com/articles/SB10001424052702304066504576345553135009870.

Wolfgang, Marvin E. 1958. Patterns in Criminal Homicide. Philadelphia: University of Pennsylvania Press.

Xie, Min, and Eric P. Baumer. 2018. Reassessing the breadth of the protective benefit of immigrant neighborhoods: A multilevel analysis of violence risk by race, ethnicity, and labor market stratification. Criminology 56: 302–332.

Zimring, Franklin E., and Gordon Hawkins. 1997. Crime is Not the Problem: Lethal Violence in America. New York: Oxford University Press.

Zimring, Franklin E. 2007. The Great American Crime Decline. New York: Oxford University Press.

# Cambridge Elements ☰

# Criminology

### David Weisburd
*George Mason University, Virginia*
*Hebrew University of Jerusalem*

## Advisory Board

## About the series

Elements in Criminology seeks to identify key contributions in theory and empirical research that help to identify, enable, and stake out advances in contemporary criminology. The series will focus on radical new ways of understanding and framing criminology, whether of place, communities, persons, or situations. The relevance of criminology for preventing and controlling crime will also be a key focus of this series.

# Cambridge Elements ☰

# Criminology

## Elements in the Series

A full series listing is available at: www.cambridge.org/ECRM.

Printed in the United States
by Baker & Taylor Publisher Services